T0196872

When Soul Is Life

*Life Transforming Wisdom
from the Heart of the Soul*

Kylie Riordan

BALBOA.
PRESS

A DIVISION OF HAY HOUSE

Balboa Press books may be ordered through booksellers or by contacting:

Balboa Press
A Division of Hay House
1663 Liberty Drive
Bloomington, IN 47403
www.balboapress.com.au
1 (877) 407-4847

Because of the dynamic nature of the Internet, any web addresses or links contained in this book may have changed since publication and may no longer be valid. The views expressed in this work are solely those of the author and do not necessarily reflect the views of the publisher, and the publisher hereby disclaims any responsibility for them.

The author of this book does not dispense medical advice or prescribe the use of any technique as a form of treatment for physical, emotional, or medical problems without the advice of a physician, either directly or indirectly. The intent of the author is only to offer information of a general nature to help you in your quest for emotional and spiritual well-being. In the event you use any of the information in this book for yourself, which is your constitutional right, the author and the publisher assume no responsibility for your actions.

Any people depicted in stock imagery provided by Thinkstock are models, and such images are being used for illustrative purposes only.
Certain stock imagery © Thinkstock.

Print information available on the last page.

ISBN: 978-1-5043-1136-6 (sc)
ISBN: 978-1-5043-1157-1 (e)

Balboa Press rev. date: 11/17/2017

Contents

Dedicated to my Abuelo…

Your Light always shone the brightest and you were a pure joy to be around. I learnt my greatest lessons in love because of you. Thank you for being my Abuelo. Your love has been etched on my Soul for eternity.

'Shine your Light on Earth so bright that you leave a trail of sparkly love wherever you go, and leave people transformed by your love and kindness. May the miracle of love always grace your life and forever bless those whose lives your Light touches.'

Acknowledgements

There are a lot of people behind the scenes that make a book possible; no book comes into creation without the support and love from a lot of gorgeous souls. The truth is this book would never have been possible if it wasn't for my family. I couldn't write this book without acknowledging how blessed I am for having my family. I am so grateful to all of those who made this book possible. Firstly, to my husband, your faith, strength, and love blow my mind every day. I am grateful for the gift of your love, Wade, and with you I feel complete. I still have to pinch myself everyday hoping that it is not a dream that you are a part of my life; lucky for me, it is not. I will love you for an eternity. To my children, you have brought me a joy and love that I never knew was possible. When I was growing up, I wanted to be one of two things: either a nun or a mum. I am grateful I chose to be your mum every day, as there is no greater blessing. Blade, Savannah, and Scarlet, to have the gift of your love is the greatest blessing anyone can ask for. There is nothing you could do that will make me love you any less. I look forward to the years of joy and love we have ahead of us. You three are the reason I know what real love is. To my mum, who has always been one of the strongest women I know, and who has taught me the importance of kindness and love because of her example. I am a proud daughter and a lucky one at that. I love you Mum, so thank you for all that you do. To my little sister Connie, your friendship has been one of my greatest gifts, and I don't think I would be the person I am today without you walking by my side for the last Thirty-Three years. I look forward to holding your hand on our walk of life, and when you fall, I will be there to pick you up for the rest of my life. Without your kindness and wisdom this book would not be complete, thank you for telling me what I needed to hear. To my little brother Neil, whose kindness is such a rarity on Earth, I am proud of you, Neil. I will always look forward to our in-depth conversations about life. I feel grateful every day that I have the two of you and your beautiful little families. To all of my extended family, mother-in-laws, cousins, father-in-laws, sister-in-laws, brother-in laws, aunties, uncles, nieces, grandparents, I know love, because you have all shown me love. Thank you. A big thank you to my editor Keidi, I'm sure your job was a hard one, but I am grateful to the Universe for your gift and for giving my book the added shine it needed. A big thank you needs to go to the artist Doodlebee for creating the artwork in the About the Author section; I saw something in your artwork that moved me and inspired me to joy. I am so grateful you wanted to collaborate and share your beautiful gift in my book. To Pastor, Erin Minogue and Kane Minogue thank you for sharing your stories on Authenticity, Vulnerability, Forgiveness and Courage with me. I am eternally grateful for your wisdom and friendship and I hope your humility and courage inspire others, like it continues to inspire me. To my first spiritual mentor in this life Fara Curlewis, you will never know the impact you have on people's lives, you were instrumental in helping me to go down this path and helping me to believe in myself. I wouldn't be here today if it wasn't for your words of wisdom and soft gentle nudges that stirred the very heart of my Soul into action when I was too afraid to shine. And to the many friends and extended family that have come and gone through my life, what a gift your friendship has been. I want you to know I have never once taken the gift of your friendship for granted and I never will. To all of the people who work at Balboa Press behind the scenes, thank you for making my book sparkle and shine. But most of all, I want to say thank you to you the reader. I know how hard life can be. I also know that it is easier to pick the road that is more often travelled. The fact you have picked up this book shows so much courage and it gives me hope that the world is in fact good hands. It's much easier to be apathetic than to make a conscious choice to be a good person, and I want you to know I am grateful for your light in the world. This acknowledgment section wouldn't be complete if I didn't say thank you to my Dad, who even though I know may never read this book, and may never know in this physical life just how much I love him, but in case you read this book, Dad... I love you.

And finally, to the energy of love that constantly surrounds me and guides me, I don't think the words 'thank you' are enough... so I will honor this love by spreading it around the world, for all to benefit.

Introduction

The purpose of this book is to highlight the essential virtues and acts of love needed to bring about authentic happiness and personal peace to our everyday lives. Spiritual development is enhanced when we live and practice the virtues of love, kindness, and compassion. The information contained within these pages is from my Soul and yours. It is information you already know at your Soul level, but you are now starting to remember it consciously. Earth School is often filled with fear, pain, and tragedy. Accessing the wisdom of your Soul will help to bring wellbeing, happiness, and peace to your life, even in the face of the greatest of adversities.

I wrote this book to share the wisdom that has helped me obtain peace and happiness, and because this is the book I wish I had read when I began my spiritual journey at the tender age of sixteen. In my life I have glimpsed perfection and experienced oneness with all a few rare times in my life, and they were all during profound acts of love and kindness, rather than during the spiritual practices of meditation or prayer.

Acts of love and kindness transcend all religions, races, and beliefs. Love is our guiding Light; the sacred piece that connects us as One. Your Soul wants you to access and live with this wisdom to help you obtain wellbeing and happiness right here and now on Earth, rather than when you reach enlightenment, or in another lifetime when you have overcome your karma. Why wait?

I am sharing these lessons with you because we are all in this together. If we want an Earth that is filled with peace and unity we must begin to listen to the calling of our very own Soul. Earth's collective Soul is crying for help right now. Are you brave enough to act with love in everything that you do from this moment on?

Every day we are bombarded with information about how to obtain happiness. But how much of this information leads to true happiness, lasting happiness, the kind of authentic happiness that can't be erased even when everything is stripped from us? Or the kind of happiness that goes straight to our heart and makes our Soul sing with joy? The truth is, not very much.

We have yet to find the one universal thing that will result in lasting, long-term happiness for everyone… or at least we think so, because we have been searching externally for the answer. The answer has always been inside of us though, and the only way it can be obtained is by living a virtuous life of kindness, compassion, and love. There is no other way.

Accessing the deepest caveats of the Soul grants permission for you to shine; for you to bring forth the knowledge and love that has always been in your heart. Together we can journey into some of the most profound lessons that life has to offer armed with the power of our Soul's wisdom. It is my hope that the journey we venture on creates an abundance of joy and love, and leaves a lasting transformation that leads to our authentic happiness.

Before you begin this journey into accessing the wisdom your Soul wants you to know, please read the following sacred contract. This contract connects you to your Soul and helps you to receive the wisdom your Soul hopes to impart. It is like an affirmation in that it is purpose driven. Please take the time to infuse the words within your heart. And when you feel you are able to accept the call of your Soul to love – sign it.

I feel so honored that we are on this journey together and I look forward to entering a sacred contract of love with you. Thank you for joining me. Namaste. 'The Soul in me honors the Soul in you.'

Soul Contract

Dear Soul,

I understand that this is not a legal binding contract, but my best intentions are to live a Soul-fueled life. In every situation I will choose to honor my authentic self. I will purposefully endeavor to practice virtues of love, kindness, and compassion in every moment. I understand that this contract will be sent out into the cosmos and I ask that all beings embrace this contract with love. I know that I am filled with endless possibilities, and with every breath I take; I will endeavor to choose love.

In moments where love is impossible, I will choose kindness. If kindness is impossible let me choose empathy. If empathy is impossible let me be without judgment. If I cannot do any of these please allow me to choose forgiveness, and if today is not the day for all of the above I know there is always tomorrow. I understand that tomorrow is always a new day and I have the ability to shine my Light and to rise above judgment, malice, hatred, anger, and fear every single day.

Soul, where I used to choose fear, I will now choose courage. I will no longer look at my failures with a closed heart. I will look at my failures with courage, strength, and tenacity. I will embrace gratitude with my whole being as I understand how truly blessed I am to experience this duality life. I understand by choosing love I choose happiness and I welcome the prosperity and wellbeing that I have because of this.

And on those days where I don't choose love, where I find it hard to forgive, I understand that you are a loving Soul who still sees my perfection, even when I can't see my own.

In Love and Light,

_____*(Sign here)*

SOUL ESSENTIALS

"Your life is unfolding exactly as it must to spiritually progress. Pain, heartache, and forgiveness are an essential part of the journey. Include love and other virtues in everything you do for more clarity, insight, and flow."

Heart and Soul

> *"Listen to the call of your Soul. It speaks only words of love and joy. Connect with the wisdom that your Soul is trying to impart. Your Soul knows how special you are and only wants to bring more joy and peace into your life."*

Although this is a spiritual book, please know that I am not going to tell you what you need to do to become enlightened, because the truth is, your Soul already is. It is my hope that the information presented in this book will show and inspire you how to have lasting authentic happiness on Earth through simple Soul-fueled wisdom... the very life-transforming wisdom that is contained within the depths of your Soul.

We have been gifted with freewill, so in reading this wisdom you get to choose what information feels right for you in this book and put whatever resonates with your heart into practice. Contrary to what we have been told in the New Age Field you do not need to do Kundalini yoga, meditate intensely, or pray every day to connect to your spiritual essence. It has always been there, so you can never be disconnected. Nor do you have to eat organic, free range, GMO free, sugar free, or meat free in order to develop spiritually.

Don't get me wrong; I recognize that all of these practices are fantastic for physical health and spiritual wellbeing, and I practice most of them daily. I do, however, believe that too much emphasis is placed on these practices and not enough emphasis is placed on the importance of acts inspired by love. The reality is, we can pray and meditate all we want, but when we come out of those moments of bliss we are presented with a reality that is often very different. When we talk about spiritual development we often skip the very human way we develop spiritually – by practicing acts of love. In this book, I present the most important spiritual virtues and the role they all play in having a life that is filled with authentic happiness, which is something we all aspire to have.

What **I AM** going to share with you is Soul-fueled wisdom that teaches how to be a good human, not a spiritual guru. It has been my experience that practicing acts of love brings a palpable joy and peace to life, and with it the spiritual development we are all seeking is obtained. There is no one on Earth who wouldn't benefit from living an inspired life motivated by love and other virtues.

At present, our consciousness lives down here in this realm, on this very real planet Earth. It is messy and vulnerable, but filled with intense beauty. If meditation and prayer is your thing, please continue with these practices because the benefits of these are ineffable, but at the same time, don't forget to access your courage to live a life filled with love, humility, gratitude, and kindness. In all my years of living and breathing spirituality the greatest truth I have come to know with certainty is that to develop spiritually we need to learn to be good humans. The process to peace and joy is pure and beautiful, but to reach this state of being, we first must embody real human virtues of kindness, compassion, love, and forgiveness.

At this present time in history we live in a very fast-paced world. Technology allows us to stream information at the touch of a button; we talk about enlightenment and spiritual development the same. We want everything now, but perfection takes time. To be truly spiritual, we must firstly be human, as they are one and the same. And being human means we will make mistakes.

The Biggest Misconception About Developing Spiritually:

- In order to be spiritual, we have to follow some determined spiritual path, follow a particular religion, be vegan, and follow a guru. The truth is, these people are no more spiritual than anybody else. Being an ordinary human who practices acts of love is all that is needed to be spiritual.

Truths About Spiritual Development:

- Embodying virtues of compassion and tolerance are essential for the peace and spiritual development of every human.
- How we fix this world is through kindness and real social activism, and not through meditation and prayer alone.
- Love is the sacred piece that connects us all as one; it is at our essence. Without love there can be no life, and without love there can be no spiritual development.

Living with Soul

All the greatest teachers in human history have taught and lived by kindness and other acts of love. They taught us the true meaning of life and this is why we look up to them with hope and conviction. Jesus, Buddha, Martin Luther King, and Mother Teresa embodied virtues of compassion, love, and kindness for all and each of them used their innate goodness to spread messages of love and peace.

If you have a deep longing for authentic happiness, or if you feel the pull of your Soul to do good, then contained within these pages are some of the answers you have merely forgotten, which through your Soul's wisdom you are NOW starting to remember. This book will help you to remember. Even if you get just one insight, this book has served its purpose.

The beautiful thing about wisdom is that every day there is something new to learn. There is an infinite power inside of you, which holds the wisdom of the ages, and this wisdom has always been available to you. Accessing the deepest caveats of your Soul's wisdom helps you to obtain the answers to some of the questions you have been seeking answers for. If you have ever thrown your hands up in desperation, your Soul's wisdom will provide you some comfort.

During the process of connecting to your Soul wisdom it is important you completely trust your intuitive filter. This is your gut instinct that tells you whether or not something you have read is Universal Truth. And remember, my truth is not necessarily your truth, but Universal Truth will always be written on your heart. When you live with your heart, you live with Soul.

Trusting Your Intuitive Filter

> *'Listen to others' guidance and wisdom, but trust your instinct. You already have the answers inside of you; others' wisdom merely helps you to remember.'*

When certain car parts are missing or faulty a car begins to stop functioning. Granted, it might work for a short time with a faulty piece but after a while it will completely break down. Take, for instance, an air filter; if your car's air filter gets blocked with dirt or dust, your engine is unable to breathe and overheats. It's a fairly inexpensive car part but its importance cannot be overlooked.

Your intuitive filter is equally important, if not more so. Without it, your connection to your engine (Soul), will burnout, breakdown, falter, and eventually crumble. If you regularly service your intuitive filter by consciously listening to the wisdom your Soul wishes to impart, the filter will prevent energetic dirt and dust (bullshit or wrong decisions), allowing for better connection to your energetic engine (your Soul).

Trusting your intuitive filter takes time, practice, and faith. It is the voice of your Soul, nudging you, urging you, and quietly blessing you if you listen to its messages. Trusting this Divine voice might require you to be vulnerable, to be courageous, and rely on the faith that your Soul has your back. The truth is, when followed, serviced, and maintained, your intuition will always lead you to the greatest Truth for your Soul, and consequently open the gateway for more expansive Soul wisdom, bringing more peace, clarity, and joy to your life.

Your intuition will not always pick the easiest route for you. It might tell you to leave your comfortable million-dollar job, sell your house, and move to the country to be self-sufficient and live off the land. Sometimes it is hard to recognize if it is your intuition or fear talking to your heart. There is no book that will tell you the things about yourself that your intuition will be able to tell you. It is your authentic internal voice and its importance is paramount when it comes to following the calling of your Soul. The wisdom that can be accessed through your intuitive filter has the ability to bring flow, clarity, and abundance to your life.

How to Gain Access to Your Intuition:

- Gut feeling: Have you ever had a churning feeling in your gut when you need to make a decision or when you are in a place that makes you feel unsafe? This is your intuition. It is stored in the brain of your solar plexus chakra, which is located in your abdomen. It's a strange feeling; almost like you have gone on a roller-coaster ride, and as you are descending there is a mixture of elation… nausea, and fear.

- Walk: Take a walk in nature and feel the energy around you. Become aware of the subtle sounds you often ignore. Anything that allows you to be in stillness and awareness and gives you the freedom to connect with your intuition.

- Shivers: A physical manifestation that your intuition uses to communicate with you often occurs via a shiver. A shiver often descends from the top of your head and goes down your spine. It feels like it goes right through you to the center of the Earth.

- Flow: When you follow your intuition you will notice that your life flows. It doesn't feel like you are being pushed or pulled in different directions, and it doesn't feel messy or chaotic.

Shine Your Light On Earth

There is this beautiful being we call the Soul, which is perfect, wise, and pure… it is you. In every moment, our Soul wisdom wants to come through, to transform and create a bridge for the sacred to enter our lives. How do we begin to open up to her beautiful messages of love? How do we invite the Divine to grace our lives? How can we shine our Light super bright on Earth? These are profound and important questions with a very simple answer… By wanting to. That is all.

- You don't need to meditate for five hours a day
- You don't need to be vegan
- You don't need to be anything other than your pure authentic self

Having the desire is all you need. If you are reading this book, that desire is well and truly there. Listening and receiving the Soul's wisdom invites love to enter every corner of your life and aids in clarity and flow. Can you imagine how beautiful life would be if everywhere you looked you felt and saw love? Being brave enough to take the journey into living and breathing virtues helps you to obtain wellbeing and happiness soulfully, yet humanly.

Your Soul only wants you to be the best version of you. It doesn't require anything from you and you will not be condemned or judged if you don't make the right choices. Making a choice based on love is all that is needed. Following the voice of your Soul requires connecting to love, and using love as if you are breathing: effortlessly and unconsciously. Humans flourish where love prevails.

What if you were allowed to be yourself? Your Soul doesn't care if you fail. There is no such thing as failure, only experiences. The only real failure is not having the courage to live authentically. Always be yourself, as there is a part of you who recognizes you are not honoring your Divine purpose and your Soul always gives you the permission to be yourself. True happiness and wellbeing is about honoring your Soul's call. Right now, your Soul is calling you to come home to love. Contrary to popular belief, you don't have to be religious or spiritual to encompass the true essence of life. Kindness, compassion, and love can be experienced by all.

> *Soul-fueled Affirmation: "I listen to the wisdom that my Soul is trying to teach. I am open to feeling fear and I combat fear with courage and strength. I believe in my innate goodness and Divine goddess/god."*

Lessons from the Heart of my Soul

Throughout my life, my Soul's wisdom has been a blessing. My life story is not very interesting. In fact, it is fairly boring. This is why I have chosen to write nonfiction for my first book instead of a memoir. I have not gone through dramatic life events resulting in a major epiphany and spiritual awakening. The catalyst for my spiritual growth has been during fairly ordinary, almost mundane moments of kindness, compassion, and love. The wisdom of my Soul knows that the gift of kindness, compassion, and gratitude is the key to accessing the love that binds us all together and it is our Divine connection to All That Is.

I have spent the last twenty years researching spirituality topics, undertaking spiritual practices, doing workshops, and attending courses. I have read hundreds (maybe even thousands) of books on self-help, religion, healing, energy, Near Death Experiences, auras, consciousness, neuroplasticity, angels, virtues, religion, Psychology, Philosophy, NLP and Clinical Hypnotherapy – the list of topics and subjects is endless.

The research was food for my Soul, but what I was really searching for was the fuel to light the fire within my Soul. I was searching for true happiness and wellbeing through all the things that spiritual people do, such as meditation, eating organic, prayer, and so on. These practices brought me the deepest of peace, but my physical body was yearning for more... more of what you ask? Human connection. I wanted to feel the same oneness that I felt through prayer and meditation but here on Earth. I no longer wanted to escape this experience.

During my life, the moments that have brought me the most peace and the deepest sense of knowing are the moments that are real, authentic, and raw. During these moments I had to learn to open my heart and be completely vulnerable. I'm not going to pretend it was easy, but it was definitely worth it. Experiences such as the unconditional love I felt when my children were born, deep compassion for a family member when they had a severe car accident, and during the profound grief after the death of a loved one taught me how to love fiercely, to be kind, and to live with compassion.

These are the moments where I have found snippets of my Soul's wisdom. I had the distinct knowing that to be truly spiritual a life must be filled with love, kindness, and gratitude, even in the face of adversity. Like breathing, I began to realize that virtues are essential not only for a human's wellbeing and happiness but for life itself, without love, life is non-existent. The moment that I listened to the calling of my heart to love, the wisdom from my Soul poured through me. Like anything that overfills I had a need to release this wisdom, and the only way to do this was to share it with the world.

My Soul's wisdom had touched the very part of my heart that I had been searching for. No longer is my journey about how bright my aura is, how much I can talk to my angels, or heal someone at a subconscious level. My life is now about finding ways to touch the lives of others through pure acts of love and kindness. It is no longer about my predetermined success or what others deem as success. It is about helping people. I am sure my connection is brighter and my aura is more beautiful because of this, but to be perfectly honest it doesn't matter to me anymore.

Life works in mysterious ways. When I began to release the expectations I had of myself in developing spiritually, I entered a state of being where moments such as changing a diaper brought me more joy and peace then being in the presence of a spiritual guru. I learned that simplicity has the ability to yield profound spiritual growth. I have felt a deeper connection with loved ones than through any prayer. I have felt the real presence of grace during moments of deep connection with my fellow humans.

Every moment is filled with grace. Once you feel this grace it becomes less important to develop spiritually and more important to be right here right now amongst the chaos, because this is where we get to experience the ultimate love and the dualities that come along with it. If you are present in each moment, you can have profound spiritual experiences during normal human moments. When we talk about the most spiritual people in the world, we think of people such as Mother Teresa whose heart was so big it overflowed with love.

Soul-fueled Affirmation: *"I now make kindness my religion, empathy my form of meditation, and compassion my prayer. I want to feel a deep connection with all sentient beings. My heart is opened for love and kindness and I will leave these as my legacy."*

2

LOVE

"Love more deeply today... just because"

The ESSENCE of LOVE

"We are all a part of the same living Universe. What
we say, think, and feel affects every single one of us. Be
mindful to always choose Love."

I am going to start right at the top with the first piece of Soul wisdom… Love. It is the most beautiful topic and the wisdom we need to understand and embrace before we can continue onto the other lessons. Even the word love is so powerful I can feel my heart burst simply by saying it. Can you feel it in your heart? When I write the word love I am talking about Divine Love; the love that is at our very Soul essence; the love that shapes us and becomes our inherent guiding light; a pure love that is ineffable and unconditional, and requires nothing from us. Call it God if you will, Source if that takes your fancy, or even the Universe. Whatever your heart connects with. I like to call it love because that's what I feel when I connect with this divine source. This love contrasts a bit in comparison to the romantic love we envision when the word love pops up.

Romantic love is one of our greatest sources of love on Earth. It is fun, exciting, joyful, and filled with an abundance of passion; however, culturally it requires something from us, such as faithfulness and so on. Divine Love requires nothing from us and can be found at the very heart of our Soul. It is the love we feel when we see a newborn baby for the first time, when we love our partner unconditionally, and when we see a beautiful sunrise.

This Divine Love is the same love that shines through in our passions and in all of our interactions, whether friendship, parenting, or community. Our Soul yearns for us to come from this place of love and experience it in all that we do. Love is something we can all do regardless of our faith, gender, religion or nationality. Love never discriminates and it is available to all.

The Emotions of Love

"Love is the most powerful emotion in the Universe, because it is the Universe."

Love is one of the most talked about themes on Earth. Unlike emotions that come and go, love is a constant, even though it changes in intensity, it will always remain a constant in our lives. People make most of their decisions based on love. Songs are written about love and most of the greatest movies and books of all time are about love in its various forms. Love is the grounding force for life. It is what inspires us to learn, to grow, and to evolve. With love and through love we get to experience some of life's greatest teachers – anger, sadness, joy, elation, passion, courage, fear, happiness, and ecstasy.

Through these emotions we learn the importance of love. The reason we endlessly search for the 'perfect' love that never hurts us or allows us to feel sadness. At some point in our beautiful lives we will inevitably know loss and/or sadness because of love. This loss and sadness is proof we are blessed because we have experienced a love that is so grand it hurts when it is 'lost.'

The Truths of Love

The first truth is, love is never lost it just changes form. Love continues to exist... long after our physical life is over, and long after a relationship breaks down. Love is the strongest energy; it radiates from the core of our Soul and connects us as one. Even if love has 'hurt' us, it is better to have loved and then we use that feeling of love as our everyday guiding force, rather than to be lost without love.

The second truth is, love **NEVER** hurts. It's the fear of losing love that hurts, the absence of love that makes us ache the most, and it may even be the conditions imposed from others that hurts, which is never truly love. What hurt us the most are the acts we do when we are afraid.

The third truth is that life is always leading us into experiences where we get to feel deeper love. These glimpses of grace are gifted to us daily, but we have to be open in order to love to see the gifts that are presented to us. If your heart is open, you can be sure that each day gifts of love will be presented to you. Are you courageous enough to seek out these beautiful gifts of love even when faced with the fear of vulnerability?

Every moment in life is leading us to love, that's why:

- Kindness enriches the Soul
- Laughter fills our heart with spiritual putty
- Compassion is our greatest blessing.

It's the simple things in life… such as the richness of love that brings us the greatest joy in life. Love allows us to see life's greatest artwork on display in our everyday lives. When we see this artwork our souls are forever enriched. Our Soul shines at its brightest when we express love, and because we are wired for love it feels awful when we live outside of this natural setting.

Courage in the Face of Love

When we have lived a large portion of our lives in fear it is sometimes hard to live with love. The fear of being hurt by love should not stop you from feeling love and embracing love. Eventually, if love becomes our default setting, we begin to live every day with a love so strong it sends waves of love to those who don't have the strength to love.

At the beginning, love requires consciously moving past fears, and placing yourself in potentially vulnerable situations. If we begin with loving consciously... it soon becomes an unconscious action and your natural default setting of love kicks in. Not only do you benefit from this, but the whole world benefits too.

The road to love always ends up at the destination of love. The beautiful thing about love is that it takes great courage. It takes persistence, tolerance, and faith and it is one of our greatest teachers. Love is how we build a generous heart, because to love unconditionally requires you to be generous with your love, time, and compassion. It encourages us to love even when we don't think the person deserves our love. Unconditional love requires us to be creative in the way we love even if it pushes us past our comfort zone.

What Authentic Love Looks Like

Love doesn't always look perfect; it can often be messy, and as humans we are filled with 'imperfections,' however these apparent imperfections create our uniqueness. Sometimes love is hard, especially when you are not ready to release something that does not serve you. When I find love to be hard, I try to be kind.

If kindness is impossible, and sometimes it will feel that way, try again tomorrow. People often forget that each day is a new chance to love and to spread our kindness. It is better to love even if only for one-day than to close one's heart because of guilt or fear.

Guilt and shame serve no purpose other than to make us feel bad and they keep us in the space of undesirable behaviors and fears. The more time you spend in the space of love and kindness, the easier these spaces are to fall back into. It is like a snowball effect. Over time, the more you practice love you begin to spend less and less time within the space of anger, tiredness, and stress.

It has taken me years of practicing the art of Soul love, and during these years I have had the distinct awareness that I have more love available to me in any moment than I was previously able to even imagine. I also realize I am far from perfect, but the realization that my imperfections create a stepping-stone for me to be courageous, and to learn to transcend fear has helped me learn to love the very imperfections I used to hate.

The greatest truth is that love is always enough. I know we have been fed the lie that it is not enough, but this was created on the notion that love was flawed and comes with conditions of perfection. When we feel love is not enough, often we are not being authentic to ourselves. In western culture, romantic love particularly seems to be shadowed by pre-conceived perceptions and falsifications, but authentic love requires you to connect to the heart of another at a Soul level… Authentic love requires you to access the hidden wells of talents that enable you to connect at a conscious level and to love without conditions.

More Love:

- When needing to make a decision, always choose one that brings you closer to love, because it will lead to a life filled with much more happiness, clarity, and flow.
- We all have a purpose in life, and although all life purposes vary, the one thing every Soul is here to do is spread love. In moments where it is hard to find your purpose, be aware of our collective purpose and align with the power of love.
- Always try to speak words of love. People often remember the words that hurt the most, but words of love leave an imprint forever on their Soul. We have the innate power to leave the world in a better place because of our ability to love. I believe when we die we have to view every moment of our lives and how those moments affected those we interacted

with. Imagine if at the end of your life you got a watch a movie that was filled mostly with love?

- Enter into the hearts of others by removing judgment and any imposed conditions about how people should be. Try to understand every single person's life, choices, and actions directly through their eyes. Develop compassion and know that every single person on this planet has his or her own heartache. We are all facing an unseen battle that most people know nothing about. Even the people who commit the most heinous of crimes have pain and heartache in their heart. We may never know what they have been through. Compassion enables us to connect to the very heart of another Soul, and it is hard to judge when you connect at a heart level.

- Instead of getting angry with someone or judging him or her when they hurt you, pray for them. Prayer is a form of love and by praying for them you will give them the gift of your love. It also releases you from attachment.

- Everyday tell people that you love them, even if you are fighting with them. Who cares if they 'win' the fight? In essence you are the winner because you were the one who used love to combat your fight.

- Simple things such as a gentle touch, a kind embrace or a smile softens even the hardest of hearts. We all respond to love favorably. Love quite literally breaks down all barriers. We all need love to survive and thrive.

The Fear of Love

Love never hurts. It is the fear of love hurting that hurts. When someone hurts you, it is not the love that hurts you, but the actions of the person. This fear of hurt stops people from living with a heart full of love. Because who wants to feel pain? The truth is, nobody. I know I don't. But what if we learned to use pain as a catalyst for growth, which encourages us to love even greater? I feel sad when people say love hurts, because to me love has never hurt. My restrictions I impose on others hurt me. The fear of losing someone I love hurts me. But the essence of love has never hurt me. It wasn't until I opened up my heart fully and exposed all of my vulnerabilities that I came to understand the importance of loving wholeheartedly. Life is no longer about playing it safe for me; it is about loving fiercely.

Inside of all of us is a pocket of love so pure, so complete, that it fills the void of illusion that fear often occupies. You don't need to understand love in order to love. Love doesn't require you to have knowledge of its working; it's a feeling, a thought, a creation. It is the essence of life and without it is where pain can be found. Think about all of the bad things that happen in the world. Do you think any of these things would happen if we lived by the compass of love? I don't think so. Do you think terrorists would kill if they lived by love? Do you think war would exist if we chose love instead of greed or political gain? No. I even think that natural disasters wouldn't be so prevalent if we loved the very Earth that gives us our home and sustains us.

It is our disconnection to the source of love that has caused all of the problems we now face on Earth, and not just some of them, but every single one of them. The only solution is to love. And it can start with you. What practices can you put in place in your daily life to include more love? You have an incredible ability to transform life on Earth. The day you were born, the Earth was blessed with another beautiful Soul; a perfect Soul, with a Divine spark of unconditional love inside of you. Spread that love. Know that you have the ability to transform merely by living with love.

Your life is always unfolding exactly as it must for your Soul to spiritually progress. By including love in everything you do you can be certain that your life will have greater flow and peace. Love is a footprint we get a chance to leave.

Love Exercise

1. Sit down in a quiet and comfortable place where you will not be disturbed.
2. Pick someone who you find especially hard to love.
3. Close your eyes and take a few deep breaths in.
4. Visualize the person and try to remember a time you were in the same room as them. Visualize yourself holding a wooden box in your hands in the same image.
5. Pay attention to any negative feeling about the other person you might have. I want you to slowly pick each emotion or feeling. If you feel frustration, visualize the word frustration flying into the box and do this for every feeling or thought that makes you feel angry or sad.
6. Once you can't find any more negative feelings, place a wooden lid on the box.
7. Visualize a fire in the corner of your image and visualize yourself throwing the box into the fire. Watch the embers, see the box disintegrate, feel the heat; use all of your senses to visualize the box completely disappearing.
8. Next, visualize yourself sending big beams of pink energy, transferring from your heart to the heart of the person you find it hard to love.
9. The final step is the most important – bless them, send them loving thoughts, hope for the best for them, and let the pain and hurt that used to be in your heart when you thought of that person be gone with the wooden box.

My Lessons in Love

I used to be a bit cocky when it came to love. I thought I knew what love was, the real love, which is unconditional and infinite. It doesn't take much to strip the cockiness out of people when they are thrown into life-changing moments. My life-changing moment was the birth of my first child, and everything I knew about love was null and void in a spilt second. Holding my firstborn son Blade for the first time, the love I felt poured thorough my entire being and created a feeling of bliss. This intense burst of love infused every cell in my body and left me wanting to replicate that love. The love I felt in that moment took away all of the fear that had previously taken space up in my heart and helped me to feel comforted and to know with certainty that I had just experienced a Divine presence of love.

It was peaceful and electrifying at the same time. The pure love I felt gave me my first snippets of Soul love during this physical life. I knew with certainty, by holding a pure Soul who had not yet been tainted from the pain of Earth, that our source is love. It made perfect sense, and for the first time in my life I knew what love truly is… not fake love… not romantic love… but Divine Love, the source of all love. For the first time in my life, I understood the very meaning of life and it was like volumes of wisdom and Universal Truth was available to me.

After experiencing this love, I needed to know how I could have and experience more of this love in my life. It became my mission to only do things that would make me feel that love again. Unfortunately, I had to stop at three children otherwise my husband would probably divorce me, so I learnt to replicate this love in all areas of my life. We have all been blessed with brief snippets of this Divine love… this love, if we live and breathe it, can become the gateway to everlasting happiness.

When a newborn baby comes onto Earth, there is only love. It is palpable and that is why even the toughest men crumble when they see a newborn baby. This is the love I felt. This same love we feel when we see a newborn for the first time is the very love that is at the core of every living Soul. We have just covered it up with human garbage. You don't need to have a baby or see a newborn to understand and feel this ultimate love. There are moments of divinity everywhere you look. All you need to do is align with the energy of love to be able to see its miracles in everyday life. You can't expect miracles if you don't look for miracles, and if you don't search for the Divine in the ordinary moments, you will never find the Divine in the extraordinary.

Some people need huge awakenings such as a near death experience to learn to understand love. The truth is we don't need to experience the trauma of an accident or an illness to see what is Divine right in front of our eyes. Millions of people who have reported having a near death experience have all said that this life is just an illusion. When you die, you are surrounded by love, you are love, and you know you will always be love. You don't have to experience lessons of love in such a traumatic way though. Be open to living and breathing love from this moment on, and make a conscious effort to love with every breath you take. Watch as the miracle of love begins to grace your entire being.

Right now, place your hand on your heart and take three deep breaths in. Breathe in pain, hurt, fear, and anger. Breathe out love. Focus on the out breath. Focus on the love that is in your heart and feel it expand. After you repeat this exercise three times try to tell me this airy-fairy lovey dove stuff isn't the most fantastic feeling you have ever felt in your life? You can't, can you? There is no denying the Truth.

I feel sad when people tell me to 'go do my Love and Light 'shit' and I'll face life head on and deal with the real problems.' It is like they believe I can't see what is all around me. Don't worry, I can, however I am just solution focused not problem focused. You can't fix a problem with the same problem that caused it. With certainty I know that the Love and Light 'shit' is the only way the real problems will be solved, because to love wholeheartedly is the harder option, but it is worth it.

The proof is in the pudding when we love, it feels good and everybody wins. Love and Light really is the solution. I'm not saying bad shit doesn't happen. What I am saying is that love is the only way to get rid of that bad. When a Soul is born they are pure love. But then life gets in the way and depending on how hard their life has been and how much love they have been shown, results in how their life turns out… a life graced with love is a life filled with joy. It will still be filled with pain and fear, because this is where the lessons in life can be found, but love will give people the strength, tolerance, and resilience to face any adversity life throws its way.

The Only Thing I Know for Sure

There are things I know and there is one thing I know for sure. Love.. Authentic love that encourages loving others regardless of who or what they are, how they fit into our lives or how they treat us. It is a love that is wrapped with kindness and encourages compassion and forgiveness. To love wholeheartedly is what we must all aspire to.

To love your child is easy, but to love someone who has wronged you is extremely hard. This is where most people find it hard to love. Loving someone doesn't require you to accept what he or she is doing; you can still love someone and disagree with what they do, and you can still love someone even if they cannot be in your life anymore.

Humans always come up with excuses about why certain people are unworthy of love; these are just excuses that validate our ego, because the truth is, every single Soul is worthy of love. Learning to love in the hardest of circumstances in our lives is where opportunities for growth are gifted to us, where we get the chance to shine our Light the brightest, where we learn to transcend anger, malice, jealousy, and rage, and turn them into the complete opposite emotions.

Now I can already hear a few of you say there a few 'filthy' people on Earth who are not worthy of love. I want you to reflect for a minute and connect to your Soul. Don't listen to me if you don't believe me, and that's okay, as my truth may be different to yours…

but I want you to ask your own Soul wisdom. Do you honestly believe that even the worst person on Earth is not worthy of love?

Think about this question for a moment… Is even the worst person on Earth worthy of love? They are. How do I know even the worse person on Earth is worthy of love? Because the sad truth is, most of the time the people who commit the worse crimes are those who have not experienced authentic love. So to not love them is to turn them into the people they are today or even worse. Because without love people are unable to flourish, to grow, to bloom, and they will begin to lose the connection they have to their Soul, which tells them, what they are doing is wrong.

Behind every back-story of a criminal is someone who has not received loved or someone who has been led to believe that they are less than perfect, less than pure. Take for instance Charles Manson. When someone says his name it mostly conjures up images of the devil in the minds of those who hear his name. What he did was unimaginable and he shocked the very core of the western world. In the majority of peoples minds it's easy to pigeon hole him as one of the worst people in human history. What's hard to imagine though is at one point this man was a child, an innocent child who only ever wanted to be loved, the same as every other child.

I was saddened to hear that as a child, Manson's mother sold him for a pint of beer at the pub. Can you imagine the type of isolation; loneliness and unworthiness a child would feel if their very own mother gave them away for a beer? Now it's not hard to see how Manson turned into the man he became.

Without love, that poor child had no hope but to turn into the troubled man he became. Love is our guiding force, without it we loose our connection to the part of us that tells us what we are doing is wrong. This is the only way another Soul can hurt anyone. Yes, what he did was terrible and yes by being the man he turned into he destroyed the lives of copious amounts of people. There is no denying that what he did was evil. But it proves that you can take what you want from someone, but if you take away love you take away the very essence of a man.

This is how I know every Soul is worthy of love because it is the lack of love Manson had in his formative years that turned him into who he became. What part can we play in preventing this in the future? Love. Our job is to add as much love to the world as possible. Our love might the piece of hope that someone sees or feels that steers them towards the light and away from darkness. Tell a Soul he's beautiful and full of love watch as he unfolds into love.

I know that this type of love does not come naturally to us. However, you can learn to still love, even if you can't acknowledge it out loud, or you can't tell others or you can't even admit it to yourself, it still transfers the energy of love to them. At a Soul level it replenishes them and gives them a love they may never have experienced in this lifetime. Our judicial system has yet to prevent crimes, and unfortunately crime is on the increase. We haven't tried love yet. But if this love is hard for you at the moment then first try to increase the love you have for your friends and family.

Love will always be the most important language spoken in the home. We are not always going to be nice. We are going to make mistakes, we are going to do things we may regret, but if we constantly turn to love, we will head in the right direction, even if we have to slow down and go over a few speed bumps along the way. The meaning of life can be summed up in one very little but hugely significant word… LOVE. Be love. Live love. Embrace love.

> *Soul-fueled Affirmation: 'Where I used to choose emotions, such as anger or malice, I will now try to choose love, and if I notice these emotions well up in me, I realize I can make a conscious choice to choose a different emotion, which has the ability to move me into the heart space of love. This is where I want to be.'*

3

KINDNESS

"Do something kind today. Even if it goes unnoticed, even if it is not appreciated, know that your Soul remembers and will beam with love. Your kindness matters.'

Kindness: The Bliss Maker

"Kindness is like a boomerang; it always comes back to
you in the most unusual Divine way. Kindness is the
stuff that magic is created from."

After love, the second most important Soul lesson is kindness, and
those of you who follow me on my social media pages will already
know I have an addiction to writing about kindness. In my eyes
there can never be enough kindness in the world. It is my goal to
make kindness spread like a wildfire through the world and to be
a catalyst for kindness. I also hope that through accessing your
Soul wisdom on kindness you will want to become a catalyst for
kindness also.

Kindness is pure living energy and the stuff that greatness is
made out of. Kindness is often a simple act, which doesn't need to
cost a single cent, and it can be truly life transforming. Kindness
can be used as a stepping-stone to learn to love, which is our greatest
virtue. Often love is a harder virtue to master but kindness only takes
practice and it can start very simply.

Kindness isn't only an act that is forgotten and released into
the ethers after it is done. Kindness goes well and truly beyond the
act, in that there is sacredness to it. When performing an act of
kindness, you are admitting that you are one with another Soul. In
a moment of kindness, you are putting someone else first, which
is a beautiful Soul lesson and essential to spiritual development.
When you are being kind you are only thinking with the brain of
your Soul, rather than the ego brain that primarily used to meet
your needs only. An act of kindness helps you to remember that
essence of love you were inherently built from which connects
you to the Divine.

Kindness is a common theme in all major religions and
philosophies. The guiding foundation of all the major religions is
kindness and love. All religions have beautiful messages of kindness

to teach. When we begin to see the same underlying messages they have in common, we will get closer to unity. There is no other shortcut to unity. We have to focus on the beliefs we all have in common, not our differences. Instead of using our religions as a form of separation, we need to align the core values of each individual religion and use these virtues as our weapon of defense.

Because kindness is at the core of all religion, from a Soul perspective it really doesn't matter what religion you follow. What matters is how you treat another Soul. Practicing acts of kindness allows divinity to shine through in all that you do. A kind Soul radiates beauty; you can see it in their eyes. A person who lives kindness is aligned with the universal wisdom of oneness, regardless if they are spiritual or religious.

Kindness is a virtue that for the most part has come easy to me. We all have that one virtue that doesn't take as much effort as the others. I have always lived to be kind. I have always wanted to see people smile, but like most people I was selective to those whom I was kind to. It was only ever people I deemed 'worthy' of kindness who received my kindness. It has taken me a number of years to release my attachment to selective kindness.

I don't need to know the other person's story anymore; regardless of who they are or what they have done, kindness is still essential. I now look for opportunities to express kindness everywhere, and often I am kinder to the people who don't seem worthy of kindness, because I am aware that these people need to experience kindness the most.

Kindness doesn't have to be extravagant. Something as simple as a smile has the ability to transforms someone's day for when you smile you're entering into a sacred contract with love. A smile gifts someone with hope and aids in connectedness. Without a doubt, it will always brighten your day too, which helps. I believe a smile is how angels communicate. It transcends language, nationalities, and even species. It is an authentic representation of your soul essence.

Authentic Kindness

I am one of the lucky few whose been on the receiving end of an act of authentic kindness. Once you have experienced this kindness, you will always want to embody kindness and become a beacon for this virtue, there's no turning back. Authentic Kindness when experienced is divinity in action. It takes you away from yourself; it gives you hope and glimpses of the sacred. This authentic act of kindness that I received, was only one simple act, I'm not sure if the person who was kind to me was even aware of the impact they had on my life, but their act of kindness transformed me at the very core of my heart.

The moment of kindness shaped me into the person I am today. Because the way I felt in the moment of kindness was so profoundly loved, I needed to share this love with other people, so that they could be blessed with the same feeling of love and grace that I experienced. I truly felt more love and grace in one simple act of kindness than through any spiritual practice before.

This act of kindness was at a mediation retreat. I was on my fifth day of a ten-day silent mediation retreat. On the morning of the fifth day whilst I was getting up for our four o'clock mediation in the common hall I began to feel gravely ill. Committed to my meditation practice I attended the mediation for a short while. However, the ill feeling only intensified so I headed back to my room to continue my meditation on my bed in the hopes that I might feel better.

The mediation was going well until out of nowhere, without warning, I felt a big thump in my chest. I had experienced this a couple of times during my life so it was not new, but even so I was deeply afraid in the moment. I tried to stand up to get help and as I stood up I collapsed on the floor and passed out. When I came to I was lying on the floor, shaking and very much needing to go to the toilet but I didn't have the strength in me to move.

I lay on the floor for what seemed like hours, alone, scared. In reality it was only a couple of minutes until my roommate came back and found me and ran for help. Once everything was sorted out and they arranged for my husband to come and pick me up they sent the manager over to sit with me because I was still feeling very unwell. Although I had seen the manager a number of times during my time at the retreat I had not spoken to her or made eye contact, as it was one of the rules of the retreat.

The manager didn't know me. I didn't know her. In the hour that she sat with me, my life completely transformed from that of fear to love. I had never experienced compassion and kindness like this lady had showed. It was authentic. I'd like to say that she did something spectacular, she didn't really, the love, kindness and compassion was built into her. I felt it. I really felt it. She had this presence about her that didn't need words. But when she spoke to me I felt like I really mattered to her, she showed compassion to me, that I had only ever read about it books. And radiated a love that was truly palpable, a love that came straight from the heart of her Soul.

I came away from this experience with a couple of life changing truths. The first truth was an instant knowing from that day on that it was my job to help other people to feel the same way this beautiful soul had made me feel. I wanted other people to also be blessed with a spiritual experience of authentic love and connectedness. I felt it wouldn't be fair for me to keep such beauty to myself. The second truth was that although I knew mediation was essential for wellbeing, happiness and connectedness, I never realized that human connectedness through acts inspired by love could be so life transforming.

The fact that I hadn't had the chance to connect heart to heart with this beautiful lady before meant I was truly missing out. I never got to see the true representation of love in her eyes because I was caught up in becoming a good meditator. From that moment on I knew the importance of real human connection. I knew then that I needed to stop researching spirituality topics and looking for the perfect mystical experience. It was time for me to put authentic kindness into action.

Kindness is Essential for Wellbeing

In our western culture, we are misled to believe that money will bring you happiness and the weight loss industry makes bucket-loads of money trying to get you to believe that happiness can be found in having the perfect body. But what if the very happiness you have been searching for comes via something as simple as living kindness, compassion, and love?

There is no money to be made from kindness. There is nothing to sell you, but you can be sold on the fact that kindness is the secret ingredient to have a truly authentically happy life. When you are kind, your heart sings and it sets your Soul on fire, and then your life is changed from the inside out, your heart expands and resonates with universal love. There is no drug in the world that could recreate the feeling of pure bliss that an act of kindness creates, and no weight loss program for that matter. Focusing on how you can be of service in the world takes you away from the self and puts you in the direction of connectedness.

A true act of kindness is the fuel to light the fire of love within your Soul. It's the stuff magic is made of and the true representation of Divine Love. It really is life transforming when you are kind to another Soul; a pure joy pervades your life, all because you gifted a piece of your heart.

Next time you watch an advertisement about a new weight-loss miracle, before you bite into self-loathing, think about a random of act of kindness you can perform (or the Bliss Maker as I have termed it), no matter how small. Change your focus to that of service. Replace self-loathing with kindness and make kindness your fallback.

Let Kindness Be What You Are Remembered For

Let your kind heart be the very thing others remember you by. Kindness lasts an eternity. It is something that can last long after youth and beauty fade, and it becomes a blessing you can leave to the world. A kind Soul radiates the most authentic beauty, so to let your authentic beauty shine through, all you need is kindness. We get told every day to exercise to keep the body fit and healthy. I think it is equally important to remember to exercise your kindness and to increase the brightness of your own Light; this is essential for your own spiritual wellbeing and for those special souls that your kindness gets to touch.

It only takes one single bad act to destroy thousands of lives. A good act goes hand in hand. It takes but one good act to transform and inspire thousands of lives. Our kindness has the ability to help others. Our kindness can be the reason someone has hope again, our kindness is a powerful gift, one that we are always capable of doing. If kindness doesn't come naturally to you, keep practicing and you will find that one-day, during a moment of kindness, you will experience a sense of peace that will envelop your whole heart. The peace will remove the illusion of pain and separation from your heart, and from this moment on kindness will become effortless for you.

If you are one of the millions of people who would like to see world peace, your Soul is urging you to be kind. Kindness is an essential stepping-stone to achieving peace and unity. It is my hope that my legacy will be my gifts of kindness that were offered to the world. Each day my Soul urges me to be the Light for another soul during their dark times. Hopefully my kindness, love, and compassion are the torch that helps them find their way.

> *Soul-fueled Affirmation: 'When I reflect back on my life, I hope my memories are shaped by the acts of kindness that I bestowed on the world, and it is my hope that because of these acts, thousands of lives were transformed.'*

Finding Kindness Outside of Survival Mode

Looking back on your life, you may remember a time where you felt connected and at peace. Kindness tends to come naturally at these times, but sometimes it doesn't, particularly when we fear our own survival. The survival instinct makes us aware that we need to make enough money to fit into society and meet our basic needs. When we live in survival mode, it often doesn't allow much room for acts of kindness to grace our life.

Your Soul wisdom wants you to know that the very act of kindness allows survival to be guaranteed. Acting from a place of love allows for the sacred to enter the corners of your life that are mostly unseen. Aligning with love and other virtuous acts allows for life to flow. We must learn to develop a trust in the Universe that all our needs will be met; this is the same Universe that inspires us to choose kindness, so why wouldn't it protect us?

Now, how do we develop the trust that is needed so we can continue to shine our beautiful Light and bring generous amounts of kindness to our lives and those we have the honor of touching? Simply by letting go. Take a step back, look, breathe, and release all fear of survival to the Universe. Do it however you want… throw your hands in the air, get down on your knees, whatever takes your fancy, but affirm:

"I now release any fear stopping me from shining my Light bright on Earth. I release my ego's need for the survival instinct, and I realize this was necessary at one point in human evolution, but it has served its purpose. I now completely trust that the Universe will always support me in all that I do and I trust that an act of kindness only ensures this very support."

A good example of our needs being met and letting go is camping. When camping you need very basic items, such as a tent, some clothes, food, something to light the campfire, and a few other essentials. Nature has a beautiful way of showing us that we are truly gifted with everything we could possibly need. We don't need to live in survival mode. The Universe is abundant in riches; we just have to believe and trust that these riches will be there for us when we need them.

Once you feel you are safe and provided for, and this may take some time, let the trust encompass your entire being and watch how easy and effortless it becomes for you to be kind. Embrace the amazing ripple effects kindness has on your life. Your life and the lives your kindness touches will be changed forever.

The Gift of Kindness

We are connected to the same source of Divine Love and Light that every other Soul that exists is connected to; therefore there is only oneness. Kindness is our sacred legacy that we get to leave. Kindness is the human representation of Divine Love on Earth. When you think of kindness in these terms, when you are kind to another Soul, you are also being kind to yourself. You may need to start with baby steps, but baby steps always lead into big adult strides. Miracles can be found in baby steps. The courage to take the first step is often our hardest challenge.

I started my journey into kindness by tithing; whenever a family member was facing a particular issue I made sure I donated a small amount of money to that cause. More often than not it was under twenty dollars. I will never forget the first time I donated a hundred dollars. We were a single income family on minimum wage and one hundred dollars was a lot, so it was a crazy exercise in trust. Did I believe the Universe was able to support me and would meet all of my needs? Yes, I did… well at least I thought I did until I had to hit the donate button and then all of the fear based thoughts started to enter my mind… "What if my husband loses his job, what if we have a medically emergency or the car breaks down?" What if?

This is when I learnt the importance of letting go. I learned to develop trust through my kindness. This trust reassured me that I wasn't going to lack anything by kindness; I was only going to gain. Now, this act of kindness is very easy for me. I will happily donate without a thought of how it might affect me, because now I know with certainty that my needs will always be met and the Universe is abundant in all of its wealth. There is more than enough to go around for everyone.

There are plenty of contagious diseases that we all try to avoid. Kindness is also extremely contagious. Remember back to a time when you have received kindness? Did it make your heart beam with love? And did it make you want to go out and help someone else feel as good as you felt in that moment? Mostly that answer is yes. Kindness has to start somewhere, so will it start with you? Can you give someone the gift of your generous heart and its miraculous snowball effects?

The Spiritual Benefits of Kindness

Kindness is healing for both the recipient and the giver. When you live in the sacred space of kindness, your heart begins to expand and heal. Loving-kindness has a radiant energy, and when this is transmitted from one Soul to another the result is electrifying and palpable to those who are sensitive to energy. This pure energy is filled with the ultimate love. Energy is constantly changing and evolving and there is a real energetic connection between all sentient beings, so it is important to treasure each individual connection. Let the energetic connection be giving, loving, and joy-filled. In every moment, be sure to contribute to the purest energy… kindness and other acts of love.

Let's be honest, fashion trends come and go. What is considered hot today may very well be out of fashion tomorrow. The one thing that never goes out of fashion, though, is kindness. Without hesitation, if you asked me what the most attractive feature about someone is, I would always say kindness. Looks almost always fade with age. The real truth is that an accident or any injury can take away your beauty, but your kind heart will continue to ride any storm if you allow the stream of kindness to always have a permanent place in your heart.

In the spiritual development field, we are bombarded with information about how to develop spiritually every day, from meditating, to yoga, to green smoothies. Spiritual development is enhanced when you spread kindness and love. Doing things for others makes your soul shine and sparkle. Spiritual development is magnified when you open your heart. Be mindful to choose a vibration that aligns with your true Soul essence... kindness.

Always Remember to Take Your Heart

> *"If you are worried about the footprint that you will leave on Earth, then always remember to choose kindness. Kindness will leave the biggest footprint."*

When I was younger, being spiritual was different. It was not something people talked about and it wasn't popular, therefore I felt different. But as the years have passed by I have noticed that spiritual development along with the health and wellness field is blossoming. It intrigued me, but what has changed? Why are more people awakening? I think it is because we have come to a place where life does not work as it stands. Collectively, we are hearing the calling of our Soul, to stand up for what is right, to be a voice for the downtrodden, and to do more good than bad.

Our rules that are set in place to prevent people from getting hurt, do not work. I'm not sure if social media is one reason, but it appears people are angrier about social injustices today than they have been previously. I think we are aligning the old adage, when something is broke, we can't leave it broken anymore, and we now want to fix it.

It has gotten to the point that individually we must make a difference. We can no longer wait for governments to change. We must be the catalyst for kindness that the world needs. All that is required from us is an open heart to carry through the changes we want to see. It sounds overwhelming, but the truth is, because it is our natural alignment, when we are living and breathing kindness it feels super-fantastic. Judgment, fear, and retribution have not yet prevented people from killing each other. This is an archaic way of living. What if we tried the opposite? What if we chose kindness and compassion instead? Even when society has told us that certain people are not worthy of this?

Currently we choose when to be kind, and we judge who is deserving of kindness or generosity. The reality is, every single Soul deserves kindness, forgiveness or compassion. It is not condoning the act that they did; it is recognizing that we are all human and we fail sometimes, but we still deserve love and peace. We all intuitively know what is right and wrong. Judgment serves little purpose other than making you feel superior to another. The reality is, we are all only one wrong decision away from being the exact person we condone or judge.

It is not until we practice kindness wholeheartedly that we even begin to elevate our global consciousness and move into a paradigm of peace and love. Including kindness into our everyday life is essential for personal spiritual development; the most Divine lessons are found in the gift of kindness. When you offer kindness, you are gifting the very essence of your Soul.

Choosing Kindness

The truth is, judgment is an easier reaction than compassion or kindness, particularly if we have gone through similar events alone, and have come out the other side. It is way easier to judge someone. Judgment helps us in our need to be superior. I often hear phrases like, "I had a hard childhood and look how I turned out!" "It is their choice to choose drugs, so let them live with the consequences."

Kindness takes us out of our comfort zone, and sometimes it doesn't feel like the easier option. The ramifications of choosing kindness are plentiful and they are all positive. I used to gossip sometimes, and if I am honest, even now I sometimes find myself falling back into gossip, as it often feels like I have no control. Except I now realize it is all on me and I have absolute control over how I act in every single situation.

I thought I was "super spiritual" because I meditated, prayed, and saw people's energy. Bullocks. I was no more spiritual than the person who could do none of these. A truly spiritual person is someone who is alignment with the Divine, and is a human representation of kindness, compassion, and humility. Judgment and gossip cannot be further away from being a virtue. We all have moments where we fall back into judgment. The road to true spiritual enlightenment is about capturing those moments halfway through the thought process and feeling guilt. Guilt is not what you should feel, though. Instead, you should feel joy because you realize that it makes you feel uncomfortable to judge. Joy is the next stage.

Remember, although kindness is a choice, without kindness the world would be in a sadder state of affairs, so although it is a choice, it is also a necessity. When you begin to add kindness to your life you will get to have moments of grace so beautiful that you will know that the Divine exists with certainty. It is no longer about proving a higher intelligence/love does exist. You get to witness this Divine in moments of kindness every day in your life, which will prove with certainty it does exist. With kindness, everything is possible. When performing an act of kindness, I have witnessed in my life that something even better comes back to you, so try it today and tell me your story on twitter. I want to hear about your good fortune. Make sure you add the hashtag #GiftKindness so I get to see it. Nothing makes me happier than seeing kindness in action.

You Hold the Power

> **Instead of saying the world has so much hatred, you always have the power to BE KIND. One focuses on the problem, the other IS the solution. A problem is never fixed by focusing on the problem; we must look for a solution. Kindness is always the best solution.**

Become a Catalyst for Kindness

> *"Become a catalyst for kindness. Your kind heart may just be the courage a Soul needs to continue on their journey."*

The day I listened to the wisdom of my Soul and realized that kindness was the key to happiness, was the day I knew what true happiness felt like. I have become 'addicted' to the feel-good feeling you get when you help someone. My Soul yearns for me to help as many people as possible. Gone is the need for recognition when I perform an act of kindness. If anything, the recognition makes me feel uncomfortable. The act of kindness has become like breathing to me; an unconscious act that is essential for my wellbeing and happiness. When practiced authentically, kindness is a selfless act that is about helping another Soul without any need for a reward. It didn't take me long to realize that this kindness business is pretty special, and in true kindness fashion I had to spread the word so others could benefit from it.

One of the reasons people avoid random acts of kindness is because they have this voice inside of them that is filled with fear and questions the act of kindness. "What if my offer of kindness gets rejected? Will that hurt? I can't honestly deal with rejection." Combat that voice with courage. For every small chance that someone will knock you back, there is a much bigger chance that your act of kindness has the ability to transform, to bring Light to someone who may have lost his or her sparkle.

A lot of people in their desperation and attempts at suicide say they only needed one person to reach out to them. If one person showed they cared, things may have been different. Imagine for a minute if you were that one person who saved someone's life, because of your single act of kindness. Maybe all you did was smile at them. It cost you nothing, and took but a brief moment, yet for the other person, it was transformative. Never underestimate an act of kindness. This is real life, and it happens every day. Kindness transforms, moves, and inspires countless gorgeous souls each day.

In each moment, you have two choices:

1. To be kind, or
2. To be kind.

Any other choice feels shit (for lack of a better word) compared to the outpouring of bliss that you experience when you offer the kindness of your heart, for the pure intention of helping someone and needing nothing in return. The bonus is you do get to release feel good hormones that leave you feeling amazing. These feel good hormones leave a feeling of bliss that feels way better than any benefit you get from being selfish.

I don't know about you, but when I am selfish, I hurt, I ache, I miss the blessings that are right in front of me, and I miss opportunities to display real kindness. When we are selfish, we are only looking out for three people: me, myself and I. I don't want to regret chances of kindness, and leaving my mark on Earth. Do you?

Will you join me on my quest for global kindness by following the call of your very own Soul?

There is a perfection that lies in acts of kindness; there is a spiritual significance behind altruism, and there is science that backs up the benefits of kindness. Remember, if you choose kindness everybody wins. Briefly people's lights go out, but what if your kindness reignited their Light?

Kindness matters, for you, for your Soul, for the collective Soul, so leave your kindness footprint. We all thank you.

Ways you can be kind for free:

o Lend a compassionate ear. When someone is hurting, just be, listen, and offer your compassionate heart

o Be kind with your words – try to always speak words of love. People often only remember the words that hurt the most, but words of love leave an imprint forever on a person's Soul

o Be generous with your presence

o Try to see the good in people. Eventually, there will only be good people to see

o Be humble

o Volunteer

o Try to feel empathy instead of judgment

o Observe how you can make a difference

o Gift your time

o Gift your wisdom. We are all teachers, so leave the world better off because of your knowledge and wisdom

o Pray: Prayer is a sacred gift; it's a non-denominational connection to the source of love. It doesn't have to be formal. It is a gift of kindness that you can give without leaving the space of your own heart

o Compliment or encourage someone. It takes great courage and grace to encourage someone if you are struggling. The Universe is abundant and your time will come

o Share your gift with the world. Be kind to the world, and if you have a gift that might help another Soul, use it. The world needs your Light in it.

Personal Kindness

Back in 2015, I had the distinct pleasure of being able to volunteer for the Dalai Lama when he was in Australia. I got the job of ushering ticket holders to their seats. I took this job seriously, as I wanted to ensure that every person I came in contact with came away from my simple act of seating them, happy and hopeful for the messages the Dalai Lama would provide.

At the beginning of my first shift I had the feeling that the Dalai Lama was going to come past my door when he entered the auditorium. This gave me butterflies. Imagine being able to be so close to the Dalai Lama's energy? I still get goosebumps thinking about it. We were told he was going to enter the door on the bottom level. I knew differently. I instinctively knew he was going to come past the door I was at. I eagerly waited at the door checking tickets instead of ushering, knowing he was going to come by at any moment

Then an opportunity of kindness presented itself. A little old lady was lost and needed someone to take her to her chair. I could point her to her chair, but I didn't hesitate to take her to it, even though I knew I would miss personal contact with the Dalai Lama. I knew that if I truly wanted to embody his teaching I needed to choose kindness in this moment. And because I had received authentic kindness and I knew how good it felt, I couldn't miss an opportunity for someone else to experience kindness in action.

As I gently put my arm through hers and walked this lovely lady down to her seat, I felt a sense of peace. The kind of peace that fills that void in the space of your heart, the void you never knew existed before. This peace was unlike the disappointment I thought I would feel. This moment was life transforming for me. I chose kindness and now all I want to do is be of service and watch others smile. There is no greater joy.

As you might have guessed, the Dalai Lama did walk past our door and the other volunteers shared a special moment with him. I, on the other hand, had the most profound insight. I hold so much gratitude in my heart for the lessons I learnt from that very small (seemingly insignificant) act of kindness. I didn't get to personally meet the Dalai Lama during my two days of volunteering, but I developed an idea for this book that you are holding in your hands right now.

On this day, I had listened to my Soul wisdom, which told me to choose kindness. I had an instant knowing that true happiness comes from kindness. I learnt that my kindness continues to speak long after my voice has stopped. There is no greater blessing.

Lessons in Kindness from the Future Game Changers

Kindness is something that is naturally inside of us. The most beautiful moment I have experienced that made me know for certain we are wired for kindness, was during one of the dinner games I play with my children Blade, Savannah, and Scarlet.

The game we were playing on this night required us to each take a turn to pick a word and the person sitting next to us had to pick a word that related to each word we picked, i.e. Bread – Toast. As we were going around, my daughter Savannah said the word "human." Scarlet, aged four, was next. The word that Scarlet picked next left me speechless. She picked "kindness." Out of all the thousands of words she could have picked that related to the word human, she said kindness. Do you know why? Because kindness feels so natural to kids.

Human = Kindness
Think about that for a moment.

I don't think we are far from gaining the world peace we desire. I'm certain the younger generation have within them the power to take us to the next level of evolution, by being change makers.

Soul-fueled Affirmation: "Today I will choose to be a nice human… Just because… Because I know nobody wins in a fight… Because I understand love heals, and because my kindness has the ability to transform lives. No matter where I go in life, the most important thing I need to take with me is my heart… Always. Opportunities will always be presented for me to engage and embrace kindness, and from now on I am willing to embrace these opportunities and follow the calling of my Soul."

COMPASSION

"Enter the hearts of others and try to understand their life through their eyes. Everybody is facing a story of heartache and pain. Let them know that they are not in this alone."

Essential Compassion

> *"To embody compassion, try to remove outdated modes of thinking and judgments. Try to understand life through the eyes of someone else. Compassion is a sacred gift that gives hope."*

Now we are about to get into the nitty gritty of life transforming Soul wisdom, with the lesson of compassion. Compassion takes a much more concerted effort from each of us. Compassion and empathy can be some of the hardest virtues to master, but only because most people think they are. Most people understand love, or at least want love, and we all enjoy a feel-good random act of kindness story. Compassion is a bit harder, particularly when we feel that someone has created their own heartache, so therefore, why would we waste our precious energy on these people? We are all born compassionate and empathetic; these are part of our Divine essence, yet unfortunately along the way we sometimes lose the ability to be authentically compassionate.

The truth is, compassion is just love, kindness, and forgiveness. Compassion is the very thing we all need to feel less alone in a world that often makes us feel we are the only ones suffering. Compassion is having empathy for another Soul during their suffering, and ultimately it is our shared suffering that creates a platform for compassion to exist. Compassion is one of the surefire ways to gain quick authentic happiness in your life.

I want to add that you may never be perfect at compassion, but that doesn't mean you shouldn't try. It takes a special person to be perfect at compassion, and even then they usually lack in other areas. We are that which we spend most of our time thinking, feeling, and being. If we focus on compassion, then we will be compassionate.

If compassion is not your strong point but you are kind, focus on kindness... the more kindness you spread, the easier feelings such as compassion increases in your heart. By working on only one of these Soul lessons, by the end of your life you would have dabbled in quite a few of them, and then mostly likely you will have made a difference without even trying, and it will become your inherent nature.

You have the chance to lend your compassionate heart to those who are struggling and help make this journey that little bit easier for them, increasing your happiness in the process. There is nothing like the feeling of connecting at the heart level with another Soul who is suffering. Gifting them your time, your presence, and your compassion is often the most precious gift we can give. To be compassionate you must always try to put yourself in someone else's shoes, without judgment. The truth is, everybody has a story of heartache, pain, and turmoil; we must try to remember this in moments when compassion is hard, and often it will be.

Being Compassionate Presence

When someone is hurting, simply be with that person. It is so natural to want to give advice, but compassion is more than advice. Sometimes, the best way we can be compassionate is merely by being present. Our body language can tell the other how we are feeling. For a moment you don't need to judge, just be. Be a source of love for them and a source of compassion. Compassion helps another Soul to feel less alone, because if you think about it, the worse feeling is feeling alone. That gut wrenching feeling that nobody cares and you are in this by yourself is Soul crushing. As humans, we need to feel these Divine moments of shared connectedness so we can remember the essence of love we have come from. If you don't experience these moments during your life, your disconnection only gets stronger.

When we die, we all will be connected to the source of love and we will instantly know that we are loved, but there are often a lot of years to fill in this life. I can't imagine how hard it would be if you feel alone. I never want anybody to feel that way. Let's all vow to make others feel less alone, even if we can't identify with their story, even if we can't understand, we can understand our shared experiences in life, and sadness, fear, rejection, pain, heartache are not unique. Every single Soul on Earth will experience these at some point. This is how we become compassionate, because we understand the things we share, not the things that seem to separate us.

Put yourself in the other person's place and have compassion at a Soul level and try to remember your connectedness. It is essential for spiritual development to always be compassionate and empathetic. Living and breathing these virtues allows us to flourish. The most Divine lessons are can be experienced during moments of compassion. During such moments you connect to the very heart of another Soul, removing judgment and being completely there, minus your perceived differences.

Compassion is about admitting that you are at the same level as someone. On Earth we are taught that we are different through class, race, and religion, but at a Soul level we are exactly the same. We are all a piece of Light from the same source of Love. You can learn to have compassion for others who are different to you by working out what you do share with them. At any given point in time people are only ever doing the very best they can from their level of consciousness. When they know better they do better.

We only have control of our own consciousness, and when we evolve our own consciousness we remove judgment from our existence. We can develop our own consciousness by thinking about every act we do and think about whether or not it comes from a place of love. Ask if your action takes you closer to love or further away from love. Compassion always takes you closer; you can never underestimate the power of compassion. Compassion doesn't get enough airtime, in my opinion. Together we can make it trend.

Enter the hearts of others through the gift of compassion

Enter the hearts of others and connect with them through the gift of your compassion. When we connect with another Soul we are experiencing oneness, which brings us closer to the essence of our Soul, because at a Soul level there is only oneness. If someone else is hurting at a Soul level so are we, so if we can ease his or her pain we must. There is no escaping this pain. We may try to hide from it or deny it, but ultimately there will be a void inside of us that only compassion for another will be able to fill.

In my opinion, compassion is more important than positive thinking. We are drilled from many sources about the power of positive thinking, and yes, of course it is powerful, but do you know what is more powerful? Compassion. Positive thinking is great for individual growth, but compassion has a higher intelligence, which takes you beyond the self. Compassion helps one to be less selfish, and in a world that is filled with a lot of narcissism, it is a breath of fresh air when you see a beautiful Soul who embodies compassion.

The reality is that at any given moment we are only one wrong decision away from being the exact person we condone or judge. Instead of the place you find yourself now, imagine if one of your decisions landed you homeless. Imagine, how scared you would feel. Imagine people judging you, instead of having compassion for you. Imagine being fearful everyday for your survival, fearful that you will lack the life essentials that millions of people take for granted everyday. Imagine knowing that everyday like every other Soul you are searching for love and compassion and more often than not you are heartbreakingly faced with judgment and hostility. Imagine feeling the isolation and desperation that homeless people experience everyday.

Now imagine that this is your child, father or your husband. It's heartbreaking to imagine, isn't it? But for millions of people this is their reality it is not something they have imagined. They have dreams and hopes, like you and I, and Fears. They also have the need to be loved like you and I. If we judge their mistakes we are missing out on real chances to love them, to develop deep compassion for them. Why do we continue to do this? We must learn to develop compassion; even if we think we are unable to, we must keep trying.

The truth is we are all capable of being compassionate particularly if we understand that nobody has it all together, that people do indeed make 'mistakes' and that we don't need to be perfect, and we all have moments of anger, fear, guilt, and despair. No one is immune from these emotions, but we can all develop compassion because we have been there before and we understand the pain.

The gifting of your Soul is one of the greatest gifts we can give. Compassion is part of your Soul essence; we chose to come to this plane to assist those who are on the same walk of life. We are all in it together, and we each have our own sets of challenges that we face, and without compassion we will feel alone in all this. We are ultimately all heading in the same direction; we just face different speed humps and detours along the way. Let's guide and encourage each other at every chance we get.

Acknowledging your oneness with others helps you to have compassion for their suffering, even though it is obvious they have brought it on themselves through unwise decisions, but when you are compassionate you are no longer an outsider judging or feeling separate from others. It is not until we practice this virtue wholeheartedly from a place of love that we can really move and elevate our global consciousness into a paradigm of peace and unity.

Why Pain is Sometimes a Good Thing for Spiritual growth

Pain and suffering can teach us how to be compassionate. When your life crosses paths with a compassionate Soul you can almost guarantee that person has endured their fair share of pain. Compassion tends to come a lot easier to those who have faced adversity, particularly if they themselves were showed compassion during their time of turmoil. At a subconscious level, we all want to emulate intense feelings of love, kindness, and compassion. It is during our own hard times that we learn to become beautiful and compassionate souls. It is because we know pain that we know how to love… and often pain is a catalyst for developing compassion.

Compassion is more than feeling sorry for someone… it makes you want to help him or her to be free from his or her problems. When you feel deep compassion for someone everything in you wants to be able to help him or her out. With compassion, you ease the suffering of another person because you end up suffering together. If there were more genuine acts of compassion in the world, there would be less loneliness. Compassion often doesn't come easy and it takes motivation, but the positive news is that compassion has the ability to heal us at a mind, body, and spiritual level.

I learnt my biggest lesson in compassion through my health. I have an autoimmune disease called Grave Disease. It plays havoc with my thyroid and affects all of the systems in the body. It wasn't until I became sick that I learnt to develop compassion for others regardless of what they looked like on the outside, regardless of the brave exterior they put up or what their back stories are.

Like most people with autoimmune diseases I look perfectly fine on the outside. I have lost count the amount of times I have gone to the doctor with a resting heart rate of 150 beats per minute and the doctor is baffled because to them I look perfectly fine. This is where I gained the insight into compassion that has helped me to understand that every Soul needs compassion and it should not be reserved for the few heartbreaking stories that trend on Social Media. Compassion needs to be practiced for all. Because you never know the pain or heartache someone is hiding on the inside. You just never know, because we all know you can look perfectly fine on the outside.

Personal Lessons in Compassion

During my early twenties, I felt a bit lost, and I was in a 'poor me' faze of my life, I hated my job, I always seemed to be hung over from a night of drinking, unwell, my life was lacking spiritual nourishment and authentic purpose. I was feeling very sorry for myself. During this time, I remember being genuinely concerned that I was beginning to fall into a deep depression and I wondered how I was going to get myself out of the big hole that I was digging, which seemed to get bigger and deeper every day.

I have always been someone who has to work shit out. If there is a problem I have to fix it, not just at the surface level, but a deep Soul level. For weeks, I tried to work out why I was in the funk and how I might get myself out of it. I tried lots of thing, some too embarrassing to admit, but after a little success, I stumbled on something that finally worked, and I got myself out of the funk. I started to think about others I knew who had it worse than me, people who were facing adversities I didn't have the courage to face at the time.

This exercise helped me to cultivate a compassionate heart, well at least the beginning sparks of one. I didn't pretend that my problems no longer existed, because the truth is, they did. But I tried to focus on others. At times, this made me feel even sadder but it helped me to reduce the intensity of my burdens by thinking of another.

The truth is, true compassion doesn't come easy. It takes practice, but it is worth it. I feel deep compassion for people now even when they hurt me in the most unimaginable ways. It wasn't always like this for me, though; it took hard work. I am no different from anyone else. I am not some martyr or saint who thinks only holy thoughts. I simply know from experience that compassion feels good and there is a certain peace that envelops me in an act of compassion that is too beautiful to describe in words. I want everyone to experience this Divine bliss. Judgment and hate hurt my heart too much and I now choose to honor my heart and love it dearly; that's why when faced with a choice, I try to choose compassion.

Along the way, my Soul wisdom pointed out an insight that has changed the way I view others' stories: people only hurt you or judge you because of their own pain or fear. When you think about it that way you are not the **ONLY** victim in the situation, and instead, you become the other victim.

The Compassion Nobody Wants to Know About

Our Soul is always urging us to embrace compassion as our default setting because this is a more natural setting for us. Compassion feels good whereas judgment hurts, often more than the initial pain. Compassion is essential for world peace, and that's something we all want, so we must all work together, as each individual's input makes a difference on our collective energy.

The majority of people who are faced with horrible circumstances will have an initial reaction of pain, fear, hurt or anger. This is a normal reaction, but where we transcend the normal and work with our Soul wisdom is how we get to the next stage of healing. How long do we honestly need to stay in this space or hurt for? Long enough for the anger to eat away at our heart? Long enough for the pain to create a permanent residence in our heart, which should be opened for love and joyful experiences? No. It requires an act of self-compassion, which honors the call of your heart to love, to let go, and to forgive. Once the unwanted guest (pain, heartache) has served its purpose it then becomes a burden and outstays its welcome. And the most compassionate thing you can possibly do is let it go.

If self-compassion is hard, there is one form of compassion that is even harder and that is developing compassion for the wrongdoers. Is this even achievable? It is. On a conscious level, we don't choose how our life pans out, but we can consciously choose how we react, and your Soul wants you to remember that compassion is an essential ingredient needed to bring a palpable peace and joy to your heart.

So how do we begin to have compassion for people who commit the unthinkable? We can never control what others do, but you can be sure that the person who commits the worse crime is also a victim somewhere along the way. It is hard to imagine that the worse criminal was once a child or has a Soul like you or I… but they do, even if we wish to believe otherwise, as often this helps us feel superior, it is the Truth. Compassion for even the 'worst' of people is a virtue that most of the saints have. We ordinary folk are capable of having and honing this same virtue to the same level. Your compassion will always do way more than any judgment you have, which will only do harm.

Judgment Serves No Purpose

It is not easy to judge when you look into someone's Soul and you realize you are one with that person, and therefore you are only judging yourself. Every single one of us has a Soul and is a piece of the same collective Soul. This means there is only oneness, and contrary to what we have been taught, there is no separation. When you look at another Soul with eyes of love and compassion it is a truly beautiful gift that takes you beyond the human plane and connects you on ethereal spiritual plane. What a lovely thought that for a brief moment when we move beyond the differences and connect with the very heart of their Soul, we are not capable of judging anyone; only loving them. When you think of it this way… why do we waste so much pain on judgment, and what purpose does it serve? All judgment does is feed the ego and our need to add to separateness for power and greed, but it adds absolutely nothing positive.

There will always be moments when you get caught up in the shitty stuff, such as guilt and judgment, however begin by consciously spending less time in this space, and try to understand your connection at a Soul level. Judgment has nothing positive to offer and consequently should hold very little space in your heart. The key to successful compassion is to turn judgment into observation. Observation is a much gentler way for your rational mind to work out what went 'wrong' in someone else's life. They are homeless because they took drugs. This is an observation and you don't need to add judgment to it. Because why did they take drugs in the first place? Were they merely trying to fill a void in their life? Were they trying to wash away pain and turmoil? You may never know, and the truth is, it doesn't matter. One of your teammates on the Earth Team is homeless and the only things they need are compassion, kindness, and authentic love. Your judgment can only harm them and make them feel even lower than they already feel. Compassion is not something you are miraculously able to do one day in the future… it is a process, filled with joy if you allow it.

Compassion helps you to empathize with another Soul and grasp the shared humanity and suffering we all have. And remember, when you help someone else, the Universe remembers and next time you are down and out, you can be sure it will work its synchronistic magic so that a compassionate Soul is there to help you, too. Acknowledging your oneness with others helps you to have compassion for their suffering. Learn to feel what the energy of compassion feels like when it moves through you. Feel your heart soften and your Soul emerge.

How to be Super Compassionate

- Work out what you have in common with others, and what similarities you share. We all need food, a place to sleep, someone to love, and hope. We all have anger, malice, and fear. Try to avoid focusing on the differences that you have with others. When you focus on your shared experiences, compassion becomes a lot easier.

- Have the desire to end the suffering of someone you know who is hurting. Focus on their problems. Try to visualize the entire scenario. Feel what they may be going through and try to work out how you may be able to take their suffering away, or if you cannot take it away, is there a way you can ease their pain?

- Practice self-compassion – to be authentically compassionate requires a mastering of self-compassion. It is difficult to be truly compassionate to another soul if you can't nurture your own aching heart, if you can't feel compassion for the pain you have suffered, or if you can't feel genuine love for the strength you have showed to pull through your individual life circumstances. It's the same for all virtues, if you practice them on yourself it will be easier to transfer to others in the long run

- Listen. Be present. Remove judgment. Above all else, love

- Forgive yourself when you lack compassion. The more your practice the spiritual act of forgiveness, the easier it becomes. Along the way to mastering your skill, you will inevitably screw up. Keep practicing the sacred act of forgiveness in these moments and learn and grow from your mistakes and then repeat.

- Work out how you would like to be treated in every situation. Would you prefer to be treated with compassion and love or with distain and judgment? Once you work out how you would like to be treated, make it your goal to treat every person you come into contact with the same way you would like to be treated, no exceptions.

- To learn to be compassionate imagine yourself in the other Soul's shoes. How would you feel if that was you? Try and imagine, and feel with all of your senses. Often you will feel anxiety, or feel tears well up in your eyes simply by imagining yourself in this situation. This is compassion in action.

- Create a rapport within all of your relationships, whether it is with your spouse, friends, and/or co-workers. Try to get to know all of them, and show interest in their lives, even if what they are talking about is of no interest to you. These shared experiences often create a bond, which helps build a foundation for future blessings of compassion
- Next time you connect with someone, talk to them, look them in the eyes, and really listen. Feel what they are saying, and after they have said what they needed to say, respond only with love.

My Lessons Learnt Through the Gift of Compassion

To me, compassion for others has always been pretty easy, particularly when I hear something on the news that is utterly heartbreaking, as I feel my heart bleed for those who are suffering. The times I have found compassion hard is when I have been through a similar situation as another Soul, particularly if the situation was hard for me, and I have had no help (and no compassion) from others or myself. It was hard for me in the past because in these moments I felt like if I had to do it by myself, why can't the other person? This is not a compassionate act; I hate to admit I have been less than compassionate in such moments in the past.

It is often during our mistakes that we learn our greatest lessons. It only takes a conscious awareness of where you struggle and a want to improve that moves you to the next step and makes you a virtuous person. Your Soul is always guiding you and helping you to make positive choices. Be open to listening to its guidance so you won't miss moments of compassion in the future. We all make mistakes but the corner stone of spiritual maturity is being aware that you could have done better, and when you know better you tend to do better. There is no point in feeling guilty, as guilt serves little purpose.

One story stands out the most for me, which I have been less than compassionate in, and it is to do with mothering. When my second child was born my son was three years old. He was an active boy and my second came out screaming and didn't stop until she was four months old. I was extremely stressed and found it hard to cope with the lack of sleep during this time. My husband Wade had started a Chef Apprenticeship around the same time, and for those of you who are chefs or know chefs you may understand the crazy working hours they have. Most of the time I was home with the two children by myself.

Now I can look back with gratitude for the experience. I am so proud of the person I am and for the strength I showed. The problem lied in the fact that when I heard other mums complain about how hard they had it, I didn't feel sorry for them. I couldn't be compassionate, even though I could clearly identity with their suffering; oh I had lived and breathed their suffering. One day, I caught myself in the act of smirking when a mum was telling me her problems (at the time they seemed insignificant in comparison to my problems and I thought to myself, "welcome to my world, honey)."

This is where I went wrong. I was not listening to the call of my Soul to be present and compassionate. I was ignoring her voice. Because of the lack of compassion I was shown during this period of time in my life, I was showing this beautiful mother the same lack of compassion. And in the process, guaranteeing she was going to show the next mum that came along the same lack of compassion. But what if I was to break the cycle? Could little old Kylie truly make a difference by moving outside of my comfort zone and being compassionate? Of course I could.

By being compassionate to this beautiful mum, it wasn't going to take away the fact that I had suffered, and it made it better to know someone else didn't have to suffer the same way I did. At the heart of our Soul that is truly what we want, to end the suffering of others; even if we act differently on the outside, it's our internal desire.

Although previously I had a brief stint at scoffing at other women who complained about parenting, now I look them straight in the eyes and I empathize with them by recognizing our **SHARED** experience, and I try to offer help and advice in the hope that no one will ever have to feel as alone as I felt. Maybe my compassion has made their journey a little easier. Who knows? The truth is, I may never know. What I do know is that the lesson I learned through compassion has had a profound effect on me. I now recognize that we all form a part of the same tribe, and our tribe needs to stick together during the hardest of times. Compassion is the glue that makes us stick. I am truly grateful for the gift of this wisdom; it is my goal to listen to this wisdom every day of my life.

> **Soul-fueled Affirmation:** *"No matter where I go in life, the most important thing I need to take with me is my heart... Always. Opportunities will always be presented for me to engage and embrace compassion and empathy. I willingly embrace these opportunities and follow the calling of my Soul."*

5

Gratitude and Simplicity

"When you are grateful for the simple things in life, this is where the extraordinary can be found."

Gratitude

The Magic that is Gratitude

Gratitude is by far my favorite virtue. Just saying I feel grateful puts the biggest smile on my face, and I feel a well of overwhelming joy build up inside of me. Gratitude is one of those virtues that when said and practiced fills your heart with pure joy and peace, and when practiced enough it becomes more difficult to be angry or sad. Gratitude is one way we can obtain a sacred connection to our Soul and it is the language we use to communicate with it. Cultivating an attitude of gratitude helps to develop a deeper connection to our Soul and increases our ability to access the wisdom our Soul always wants to share with us.

With gratitude, you gain access to all of the blessings in the world and by incorporating an attitude of gratitude into you daily life it opens the gates for Divine blessings to grace your life. Gratitude is the stuff that magic is made from… actually all of the virtues are. To have authentic happiness in this life, gratitude is an essential lesson to master, and thankfully one of the easiest to start, but often one of the hardest to continue when life gets you down. Even in moments where life is hard, you will still be given glimpses of beauty so exquisite that if you are looking, gratitude will always be the end product. During hard times, our hearts are often closed to these miraculous moments, but a true master of gratitude is capable of developing the vision to see the blessing within the pain.

The Hidden Blessings in the Ordinary

Gratitude for the ordinary is a true blessing. It is easy to be grateful for the extraordinary, such as children, a new car, and so on, but the real magic lies in gratitude for the ordinary. It is a true gift, and we are given glimpses of grace in these moments. When you are grateful, you are aligning with the essence of your Soul, which only knows unconditional gratitude. In the past, gratitude has had mainly a religious association, but science is now starting to see the benefits of gratitude on our health, happiness, and prosperity. People who express gratitude are more inclined to be happier, be more empathetic, and have more joy, peace, and abundance.

Gratitude as an Abundance Creator

Showing gratitude helps us to accept what is and opens the doorway for abundance to enter. It creates abundance by shifting our thinking away from what doesn't work in our life to what **IS** working. It is how we learn to receive what we are truly entitled to. Abundance is manifested when we believe we are worthy and we can see our current blessings with clarity. I recently heard that Oprah Winfrey, who is one of the most successful women in the world, has written a gratitude list every day for the majority of her career. Is she grateful because of her success, or is she successful because she is grateful? My money is that her gratitude is the secret to her abundance.

Gratitude the Humility Teacher

Gratitude is not a form of positive thinking. It creates a shift in you that says, "I accept help, I'm okay with giving compliments, and I have humility." This can often be difficult particularly for all the martyrs in the world, and is not often thought about when people think of what gratitude entails.

It takes more than writing a gratitude list every day. To be truly effective gratitude needs to be a way of life. This is the sure-fire way to have blessings enter your life, for clarity, flow, and peace. Gratitude is a good way of connecting to the well of miracles the

Universe has on offer to you. When you say you are grateful for something... it takes on a bigger significance.

Ways to Include Gratitude into Your Daily Life:

- Each day, take a moment to reflect on how incredible life is. Look at your body, feel your skin, watch a sunset, take a walk in nature, be in awe over the miracle of birth, smile at a child, belly laugh, feel the deep love you have for your special someone, think about what makes your Soul sing. Be in awe about how incredibly lucky you are for all of this. Breathe out gratitude.
- One of the simplest ways to live gratitude is to write one thing that you are grateful for every night. Trust me when I say this… it won't be long before there are two things to write, and so on.
- If you are grateful for the food that you eat, share it. If you are grateful for the love that you get from your children, give that love back to your parents or someone else's parents.
- Today I am grateful… say these four simple words every day for profound joy and abundance. What are you grateful for today? Write it on your heart.
- Use words like thank you a lot, as it verbalizes gratitude and shows humility.

The Joy that is Gratitude

Most of the Soul lessons presented in this book are connected. Gratitude enhances every single Soul lesson and increases the impact they all have. When we are grateful for what we have, we feel a deep connection to others when they are in pain, and this helps with the virtues of forgiveness, love, compassion, and kindness. These virtues go hand-in-hand. Kindness engenders gratitude. Connecting with another brings pure joy to your life and leaves room for gratitude to enter your life. Where joy exists, you can't help but feel grateful for what you have. In moments of gratitude, you feel connectedness with others.

Eventually, with gratitude you become a magnet for what is good in the world. Your life and your heart will expand with love and connect to the fountain of universal love when you live a life of authentic gratitude, besides the divinity part of gratitude, it really does feel bloody good. Make time in your day to commit to one grateful thought; the path to greatness always starts small.

Gratitude is a true gift, because if today you are struggling and can only find one thing to be grateful for, you can be sure that tomorrow there will be two things you are grateful for, and so on. It has a snowball effect the more that you practice it, and before long, you will feel deep gratitude for the butterfly that flies by you at lunch or the soft wind that blows past your shoulder on a warm summer day.

When you really think about it, this planet gives you plenty of things to be grateful for. It's filled with enormous amounts of beauty around every corner you look, such as the sound of a baby laughing, a beautiful bird, the beach, and the beauty of summer. These things are gifted to us without us ever having to do a single thing, and even if you feel like you never have enough, your life is always lacking in something, by showing gratitude for the things you already have, you are showing the Universe that you appreciate what you already have, and you will receive even more blessings to appreciate.

Gratitude Exercise

'For grace to fill your life breathe in gratitude…
Breathe out love.'

For a moment, I want you get into a comfortable position. A safe spot free from distractions. Close your eyes and begin to focus on gratitude. You can do this simply by chanting the mantra "I am grateful" ten times. It is magnified by a thousand times when you say something you are grateful for, and a thousand more times if you can be truly be grateful for some of the seemingly mundane things people don't normally associate with gratitude, for example, your cup of coffee or the unexpected road rage you experienced because it taught you that you are still human and far from perfect.

Not everyone feels they can meditate, not everyone feels comfortable in a meditation, but sitting in a lotus position isn't the only way to meditate. Gratitude is a form of meditation and something almost everyone can do because it is as simple as saying thank you, or a moment of pure joy when you look at your children.

You can also use gratitude as a form of prayer. Gratitude aligns with the sacred; it connects you to the Divine love that is in you, and through gratitude this divinity can be accessed. So next time someone tells you need to meditate or pray and you have never felt comfortable doing these things, be grateful. Gratitude helps you to connect to a Divine presence. Meditate and pray also for added spiritual power, but if they're not for you, then try gratitude. It is simply life transforming.

Gratitude, the Secret to Manifestation

Gratitude helps you to gain greater access to the law of manifestation. It's one of the secrets that everybody talks about when manifesting. Gratitude, I believe, is the price we pay for getting life. It doesn't matter what religion you follow, if you are reading this your Soul believed in your strength to withstand the hardships this life has presented to you. You have been gifted with this beautiful experience, so look for the sacred in every moment.

With honest reflection you can find moments, gifts, and things that connect you to your Soul essence that make you feel joy and/ or love, even if these moments are far and few between. Often one moment of joy or unconditional love can carry you through ten years of pain and turmoil, they are that powerful. By focusing on those moments of joy, particularly when you are feeling negative, you will be given more moments to be grateful for. Gratitude has a power that surpasses all negative thoughts and emotions.

Personal Gratitude

The thing that helps me get through an especially hard day is, at the end of each day I know the gift of a new day is on the horizon. So, I leave what doesn't serve me anymore with the current day and embrace the blessing of a new day. The wonder and joy that can be found in the simplicity of life is gratitude inspiring. The simplicity of life can be found when you realize that at the very heart of your Soul, you are love.

Each night, when I put my three children to bed, I ask them what they are grateful for. It is such a simple act, but I believe we are never too young to learn the importance of gratitude. Sometimes my youngest will say she is grateful for the ice cream that she had that day. The smile on her face is huge and I love to see the gleam in her eyes. In those moments, I can't help but feel grateful for the smile she puts on my face. And every time I have an ice cream now, I feel a rush of gratitude because little Scarlet taught me to.

To have gratitude doesn't mean that life has to be perfect. We all know life will never be 'perfect'. I have a life that is perfect to me, I am deeply grateful for all of it. I have known deep sadness, criticism, illness, and loss. I don't really have much money. My health is terrible. And yet I am still grateful because behind all the bad there are moments of love that are so grand, so pure that make it all worthwhile. Without my illness I would probably have a successful job in business, which I know I would not be happy in. Because I am unwell I have been given time to connect, to write, to embrace moments of simplicity. Gratitude isn't about having a perfect life.

It isn't about manifesting all the material wealth our hearts could desire. Gratitude is about being thankful for the gifts of life, warts and all. Because it's in the chaos that we emerge with courage. It's in the pain that we seek growth and its within loss that we realize just how blessed we were to experience love in the first place. Love makes it all worth it.

Leave Gratitude As Your Trademark

If you are only love at your core, and eventually you re-emerge with that love… what's not to be grateful for? We only need to remember the unconditional love we have come from in order to feel blessed. To be filled with gratitude is your Divine nature and it will always align you with joy. Expressing gratitude opens the doorway to spiritual development and is a sure-fire way to manifest a stream of positivity to grace your life.

In each moment, make gratitude your trademark, and remember with every breath you take there is always something to be grateful for. The beauty that lies in each moment in life can be found in what you are willing to see. Miracles occur with every breath you take. I have seen gratitude work its miracles… it has a sublime ripple effect. Welcome the power of gratitude into your life today.

> *Soul-fueled Affirmation: 'Today I invite the powerful, transformative, and healing benefits of gratitude to grace my life, and I know with certainty that I deserve the miracles and blessings that I will receive every day of my life because of the gratitude that fills my heart. I now know, because of gratitude, I will be welcoming authentic happiness into my life. For that I am grateful.'*

Simplicity

Simply Being Present

In today's society, people are generally busy, stressed, and overwhelmed. This constant busyness leaves little room for grace to make its presence in our life or little time for relaxation, connection, stillness, and simplicity. This constant busyness creates a shift away from gratitude, where life's little blessings are held. Simplicity and stillness are often overlooked in importance for general health and wellbeing.

Boredom is healthy as it gives our mind a chance to breathe; it brings our body and Soul that much-needed sigh of relief. Creativity flourishes where boredom lives. You can find your authentic spark in a moment of stillness and simplicity. Always being busy hushes the deep voice inside your Soul that is screaming to express itself but can't be heard above the busyness that exists. Sadly, in this technological age, boredom seems to be a thing of the past. Have we forgotten the sacred act of just being? Have you been longing to feel a deeper connection to life, to have more gratitude, or to simply be more present, or embrace the blessings that can be found in each moment?

Five simple tips to help you to live in the moment:

- **Spend time in nature:** Take a moment to spend some delicious time in nature. Connect with its exquisite beauty and peacefulness; watch as you begin to feel alive after a few minutes. When you are alone in nature you understand your connection with all of life and you realize how noisy life can be.
- **Abdominal Breathing:** Abdominal breathing is the most natural form of breathing. Abdominal breathing increases

oxygen in the bloodstream, thus increasing feelings of relaxation in the body. When abdominal breathing, become aware of the stillness between each breath, as this is where you will feel the pure love that radiates in us all, where peace exists.

- **Try meditation, Yoga or Tai Chi:** Meditation, Yoga, or Tai Chi are useful tools to incorporate in your life if you are hoping to appreciate each moment. They allow you to be truly present and they help to reduce the mental mind chatter that seems to always be present, encouraging deep clarity and patience.

- **Awareness** – Become aware of your feelings. Are you tired? Stressed? Be conscious of your emotions, feel them and express them. You don't need to label them or even understand them; you just need to be aware.

- **Make peace with the past** – When you live in the past you are missing out on the peace and love that exist in the present moment. Seek comfort in the fact that the past is just a memory now.

A mind that is living in the present moment is free from the pain of the past or the worries of the future. When you start to live wholeheartedly in each moment you can really begin to appreciate the blessings that are unfolding in life in any given moment. For example, right now as I am writing this book, I am choosing to live in this present moment, because in this moment my children are at school and soon they will be home from school and there will be chaos. I think I might stay in this happy place for the time being.

Sentiment for the Soul

Simplicity is underrated in a society that claims the more you achieve the better you are. Peace can be found where simplicity exists; we must learn to aim for peace instead of success. Often, success comes easier after peace has been obtained. There is a part of you that remembers your perfect Divine spark, your true essence of pure love. Sit in stillness, remember, connect, and love. When all hope is lost and an uncertainty plagues your heart, look around at nature… she continues to exist. Stillness allows you to hear the voice of your Soul whisper words of love and messages of wisdom.

In our pursuit of success, we have forgotten how important the sacred act of just being is… this moment is all that exists. Turn the news off today. Disconnect from social media. Replace the noise with stillness, connect to nature, and fully embrace the sacred space. Today, remember to slow down and embrace every single moment. In those brief moments where you experience stillness, pay attention to your breathing, as this is where you will feel the pure love that radiates in us all. Love, simply put, is the key to happiness; if we are always busy we miss each moment of love. Joy lies in the simplicity of each moment; it's the simple things that bring us the most joy. Awareness, stillness, breathing… connectedness. This is your sacred connection to your Soul and All That Is.

We all know life has a way of quickly becoming overwhelming with the complexity of it all, but not in this moment. Stillness allows us to access the very calling of our Soul, which is often missed because of the busyness of our world, the busyness of our thoughts, and the pressures we bestow upon ourselves. Unfortunately, in a world that is driven predominately by success, along the way we have forgotten the sacred act of being. Of being completely present. Of being all of the stuff that matters, such as love, kindness, and joy.

The truth is, this moment will be the last moment you will experience this life under these circumstances with the wonderful people you love. Yesterday is the past, and the future can change in a blink of an eye. Buddha states it perfectly, "In the end, only three things matter: how much you loved, how gently you lived, and how gracefully you let go of the things not meant for you." Learn to develop a trust in the process of life and let it flow; life is constantly changing and requiring a consciousness of its process. We are one with all. Being aware of this oneness prevents fear from living in your reality. Fear only inhibits your process and denotes a separateness from all that is ultimately connected.

Stillness Exercise

Stillness can start with one simple action...

Breathe...

Right now, I want you to breathe... nothing else...
And when you finish with the first breath, take
a second one... breathe in love and joy, breathe
out pain hurt and fear.
Continue this for as many breaths as it takes for
you to feel a palpable peace.
In moments of simplicity, profound Soul wisdom
can be accessed.

Importance of stillness for dealing with stress

When we talk about living in today's western world, themes such as materialism, stress, anxiety, bullying, and the likes run rampant. Stress has an awful way of destroying lives. What causes stress? The reason that there is so much stress in today's society is pressure; we don't leave very much room for moments of stillness, we are no longer happy with the simple things in life, such as love, joy, and presence, and we are constantly searching for more. Our modern life consists of making enough money to pay the bills for the things we purchase because we think they will bring us happiness.

The truth is, authentic happiness can be found in the simplicity of life, in which is underrated today. There is a constant pressure on us to achieve more, to be more successful, to have more and more and more. In the process we deny ourselves moments of pure joy, connection and sacred bliss.

To obtain wellbeing and happiness, the first thing the Soul wants is for you to make room for connection. If you are in a constant phase of want and need, you do not leave much room for downtime, connection, and expressing joy. It's nice to see things like meditation and yoga becoming successful.

When you are constantly busy there are not many chances to notice the exquisite beauty that is all around. Connecting to nature by swimming, bushwalking, and camping is simply breathtaking. There is this overwhelming awe of nature's beautiful gifts that leaves us with deep feelings of bliss in these moments of simplicity. Whenever we finish one of these adventures with the kids, my husband Wade and I experience peace. We have a little more clarity and we are more open to feeling gratitude for the special gifts this beautiful world bestows on us. When we get home after these adventures we wonder why we don't do more of this.

During moments of simplicity and stillness, the Soul has the ability to tell you things. These moments increase awareness, and increase the number of Divine messages getting through to you from your Soul. You are able to hear these messages more easily and with more clarity about their purpose and meaning. Try simplicity and stillness today, instead of thinking about what needs to be done. Work out if any of the things on your to-do list are necessary. Instead of thinking about all the things you need to do or be before you are authentically happy, see if you have the happiness you have been searching for already inside of you. Connect with nature. Sit in a park and be aware of the birds flying around. Be more mindful of the unnecessary pressure that you place on yourself. Embrace simply being.

Watch how perfect nature is, how strong a tree is even though wind can bend it, how wise it feels, and notice what the energy feels like around you? Is there a sense of calmness? Do you notice some underlying anxiety rising up in you? Pay attention to what you feel, and allow thoughts to enter your mind, without judgment or attachment. Then allow these same thoughts to slip into the ethers. Try to pay attention to your surroundings, such as the simple but exquisite beauty of a cloud. The perfect synchronization that occurs when you look at what is and how it is all interconnected is simply amazing. It truly is.

Personal Stillness

If I could pinpoint the day that inspired me to live a life of more stillness and simplicity it would have to be the day I chose to begin to consciously live in the moment. On this seemingly ordinary day it hit me like a ton of bricks and I knew I needed to change, to be more present, and enjoy the simplicity of each moment.

My greatest lesson with stillness came in the mostly unlikely of places: a train. I have called it my train ride with Soul. I was on a business rush train and it was packed. I took a seat and placed my bag on my lap, got comfortable, fixed my clothes, and started fumbling in my bag for my phone so I could check social media. Whilst I was rummaging in my bag, for a brief moment I looked up and what I saw brought on one of my insights. Every single person on the train that day was looking at a phone or tablet, except the elderly man sitting next to me, and of course me... now.

I quickly slid my phone back into my bag. I tried to make eye contact with someone, but nothing. I tried to make sense of what had happened to society, but nothing. I felt a deep overwhelming sadness. In that moment I consciously chose to make a pact myself, a deep one-on-one inner dialogue with myself started. From that moment on I vowed to myself that I would endeavor to embrace every single moment in this life. In each moment I vowed to remember that every single morsel of this life is precious and sublime (even the shitty stuff because it teaches me to really appreciate the good stuff).

I vowed to make an effort to stop holding onto the past or worrying about a future that is still unwritten. Who cares if I'm on a train; this may be my last day, and let's be frank, train rides can change lives!

Remembering to live in the moment has made my life pretty simplistic but it has also brought me oodles of happiness. I am no longer looking for the next big thing that will make me happy, because big things only bring fleeting moments of happiness. Happiness is an internal state that requires you to be happy in each moment. How do you feel in this moment? Do you have thoughts about future events? Is your mind racing with things you need to do? How would your life feel if you were happy with what you had and needed nothing extra? Would you feel joy? Does it make you feel nervous? It is a pretty incredible feeling to be happy with what is. There is a special energy that is attracted to what is, and this energy will bring you more things in your life to be grateful for… the bigger things, but regardless, you will feel even more appreciation for the simple things.

Wellbeing and happiness needs to be felt and accessed through mindfulness, peace, and virtues. When you are connected to the essence of your Soul through stillness, you get to witness transformations unfolding every day in your life. The stillness between each breath is where you will feel the pure love that radiates in us all. Stillness is the place where you gain the courage to live your life authentically.

By the end of the train ride I was having a good laugh with the elderly gentleman next to me. We connected and it was beautiful. It was a moment of bliss I might have missed if my mind was too busy filling the space of boredom with useless information.

Courage

"Courage moves you away from fear and into moments of triumph, joy, hope, faith."

The Essence of Courage

*"Courage is a virtue that when lived makes practicing
all of the other virtues a lot more effortless, because all
virtues require courage."*

Courage is a virtue that naturally comes from the very heart of
your Soul, which means it is the very essence of your spirit. The
importance of incorporating courage into your daily repertoire of
Soul-fueled super powers cannot be understated. Out of all the
virtues, this is one of the hardest as it ignites vulnerability and it
welcomes fear. Although it is difficult, courage is a virtue we are
all capable of living. It's reassuring to know that our Soul always
believes in our strength and our courage to withstand even the
greatest of hardships and complexities in life, and our job is to learn
to develop the same faith by understanding that our life is unfolding
exactly as it must for us to spiritually progress. By being courageous
we are showing we have complete trust in the Universe to support
us in the most perfect way.

Never before in history has the world needed people who, even
in the face of adversity, can stand up and be courageous. If you want
to bring about change and transformation, courage is essential. All
virtues and wisdoms complement each other. Often love requires
courage. You need to be to be brave enough that someone will
reject your act of kindness to be kind. It doesn't matter what the
outcome, all that matters is that you chose to be kind; this is where
the courage lies.

Courage can be found underneath the lies and stories you have
been told by the voice of your fear. It might be as simple as digging
through the lies you have told yourself. Spiritual courage moves us
away from the self to realize that our purpose on Earth requires us
to be courageous to bring love and peace on Earth. Courage is a
virtue that all of the most motivational humans have. They have the

courage to be authentic, to challenge status quo, to commit to a life not limited by fears grip. We all have this innate ability to create a beautiful reality, but often this reality requires us to be courageous. The unfolding of your greatness is waiting beneath the surface for you to have the courage to believe in your power. Courage lies beyond your comfort zone, beyond where fear resides. Here lies the power that has always been inside of you.

A courageous Soul still hears the voice of their fears but doesn't listen to it. Some of the most beautiful Souls have endured great pain and sorrow. Where there is darkness, light will always shine at its brightest. Pain and trauma can be a catalyst for courage and a courageous Soul makes a conscious choice; instead of choosing to let fear win, they face the fears head-on with courage. Eventually their courage will pay off because fear will always lose the fight once challenged. Every time we face our fear we get transformed into one of those courageous Souls we admire. Often, when you are courageous and go out on a whim, you realize failures aren't as bad as you thought, and you realize there is a power to failure you didn't know existed before, and that power gives you strength. Being brave enough to show up even when fear tells you that you can't possibly be good enough is the first step to creating a purposeful life. When you feel fear make your Soul your fallback, connect to your Soul for the strength to continue, as it will always give you the strength you need.

Courage Instead of Fear

Without fear, there can be no courage, no heroes, and no moments of pure bravery. This is the duality of life. To experience the good, we must learn to overcome the bad. We all admire courageous people, as they seem to embody a super human quality that is impossible for us every day humans to embody. The truth is they don't have a special power that is only reserved for a few chosen humans; they have the same fears and vulnerabilities that every single one of us have. All they do is turn the volume down on the fear volume dial and they answer the call of their Soul when it is calling. There is a pocket of love found within the space of fear. Keep searching. Once found… there's always hope.

How can you be courageous when you are gripped with fear? The whole objective of life is having the courage to move past fear so we are capable of being the best version of ourselves we can be. Don't judge your fear; it's okay to have fear. This is a normal human reaction. Only become aware of the thoughts that ignite fear. Stillness can hush the sound of their roar; we can learn to control the thoughts.

It is easy to assume we are suffering because of a bigger picture. A life purpose, karma or life lesson is popular in today's new age field. I'm not about to tell you that these things don't exist, as they do, and we play a role in our suffering with our mental mindset. The truth is, we all need a healthy dose of negativity, pain, and heartache. It is the way we learn courage, tolerance, patience, and faith. Life is about mastering the skill of hurdling by jumping over the bad stuff. There is a certainty that your Soul is evolving in the process.

The Courage to Live an Imperfect Life

Life was never meant be perfect. The truth is, bad things happen. Trying to manifest a perfect life is a wonderful attribute and an incredible spiritual skill to master, however, there is an integral piece missing: being present. We need to develop the courage to deal with the hard times and the emotions we are presented with in our lives head-on. In today's society, we are quick to label anything that feels bad like it shouldn't exist. This only ensures that we suffer more than we are already suffering. Pain, grief, sadness, and despair are a part of the process of life. What if we need to go through these to evolve? What if they are an integral part of life and spirituality? Even though they are not desirable, they are unpleasant, and they take a huge amount of courage to experience.

Instead of running away from feelings of fear, pain, and hurt; own them. Have the courage to be present and experience these emotions, and rest-assured that emotions are always transient in their existence. Before long they will always be replaced with positive emotions and experiences. Pursuits of perfectness without being present and dealing with the underlying issues pushes down a bunch of emotions that need to come to the surface. If we continue to stuff them down there will be no more room left, one day causing a huge explosion, and this is when our engine blows up.

Along the way, the love feeling connection has been mistaken for perfection. But here is the biggie; love doesn't even require perfection to exist, and it can easily co-exist with imperfections. Life is a beautiful expression of the Divine love we came from and this is where the sacred perfection lies, not in the process of life. Life itself will never be perfect. Our job is to embrace these imperfections and to live wholeheartedly from a place of love and gratitude. Our Souls chose this duality life because of the lessons that can be learned. Venturing into courage, tolerance, and even vulnerability will teach you some of your greatest lessons.

When we make mistakes, we learn and evolve. When we realize we could have done better, we are entering a state of awareness, and in this state we can begin to live consciously. No matter who you are or what level of consciousness you have, if you are human you must deal with pain, guilt, fear, and then pervading courage. There is no escaping them. But remember, there is also, love, kindness, compassion, and hope. These gifts give us the strength to face life with courage.

Take a good look back on your life and admit that there have been imperfections rising to the surface all along. Look at the past hurts that you haven't dealt with. Know that it is normal, that imperfections are beautiful, freckles are gorgeous, weeds will always grow, a messy house means you had a couple of more minutes with the kids, a flat chest means you don't have to worry about having a sore back, and the loss of a loved one means you are a human who was lucky enough to love.

To understand courage, we must be okay with the imperfections of life. For perfection to exist, imperfection needs to flourish. This is the duality of life. The exquisite power that lies in facing the harder times (even if it means asking for help) cannot be overrated. Where the perfection lies, is in your ability to admit that although you are not perfect, and your life is not perfect, you are still blessed… with life… beautiful imperfectly perfect life. The idea that you don't have to strive for perfection is slightly empowering, don't you think? Time heals all wounds; time wraps us in a protective web by offering us the gift of tomorrow. You don't need every part of you to be perfect before you are perfect. Your imperfections combine together to make up YOU, so love all of YOU.

During my life there have been moments where I have tried my hardest to move mountains, but over time I have realized that the courage lies in moving molehills. It's in adding new layers to the molehill that mountains are created. Do you have the courage to live an imperfect life? I believe in you, your Soul believes in you… but do you believe in you?

Vulnerability

Vulnerability is a topic not many people want to talk about. Just saying the word makes most people's skin crawl. I can almost hear the voice in the head of the future readers of my book, questioning why I would put vulnerability in a book about Soul wisdom? Don't worry, I feel you; I still don't know why I added this section as it was impossible to write. The entire love chapter took me less time. Vulnerability sucks, for lack of a better word. It is not pleasant at all. But I will tell you what doesn't suck: growth, the unfolding of your greatness, courage, and following the calling of your Soul. To get to these we must learn to transcend vulnerability. There are no shortcuts. I am following the call of my Soul to write this section, because I know I have to listen to the call of my Soul. I must push past the fear of vulnerability and rejection. Because I know that pushing past the barriers that vulnerability creates in our life is one of the pieces of wisdom our Soul wants us to learn and grow through. So, this is why this section is here. Do you know how much vulnerability writing a book creates?

The courage to be vulnerable is one of the keys to authenticity, and without it we stay safe. Staying safe doesn't leave much room for becoming great. Vulnerability is the spot where courage and fear butt heads, and more often than not, fear wins because we are deeply afraid of failing, or being open and raw. Who wants to fail, or be exposed? Nobody does, but our biggest breakthroughs and moments of clarity are experienced in moments of vulnerability.

Moments of fear, rejection, pain, and hurt, are why we are so afraid to be vulnerable and the very same experiences are needed to obtain the life essentials we crave, such as self-kindness, courage, gratitude, hope, and joy. Vulnerability goes with most of the virtues and wisdoms presented in this book; we don't listen to the calling of our Soul because we are afraid of the havoc our vulnerability will play in our lives.

Embracing vulnerability gives you the ability to access a more spiritual connection or obtain deeper understanding of Soul wisdom. It's easy to get scared, but I would like to provide you with a gentle reminder that the Universe is always on your side. It always works in the most Divine ways, especially when you are courageous. Have faith that the same Divine love which, created you, is the same Divine Universe that supports you in all you do. We are all unique, one of a kind, a piece of the same light. We all share the same predisposition to vulnerability.

Because we are scared of being vulnerable, we stop ourselves from accessing the happiness we deserve by living with authenticity. To be authentic encourages you to move past fears of ridicule, failure or judgment, so you can live the life you truly deserve and desire. The only thing vulnerability can truly hurt is your progress. Although never failing is something we would all like, our Soul encourages us to remember that our job is not about having peopling liking us or playing life safe. It is about having the courage to follow the voice of our Soul, even in the face of immense vulnerability, and to live authentically... with love.

Story of Growth Through Vulnerability

I would like to share a very open and vulnerable piece of writing from my beautiful friend, Erin Minogue. It is full of Soul wisdom, brave, and contains insights into the healing that can be found in vulnerability. I felt so many emotions reading it, and I hope you do, too:

> "Today I saw someone and cried. I cried down two aisles of the supermarket. It was a sad, lost lady. It was a lady I noticed because I used to be her. Head down. Shoulders slumped, a slow shuffle, no expression, no life, and no spark or participation in life. She caught my attention as I went to get yoghurt from the refrigerated section. I happened to look down. She had no shoes on. As she moved I noticed it was a bare-foot shuffle. That's when the tears came. Not because of how she looked or because she was slow to move out of my way. It was because I felt her exhaustive sadness. I wondered what her shame was around. I wanted her to know her smile could come back and she was worthy of love. I wanted to hold her hand and tell her not to do this to herself. She didn't deserve all that hurt... guilt... shame... heaviness. She deserved to smile and have a bright future. Love. Her friends and family deserved her smile. A future filled with love. As tears dried on my face it hit me that I was crying because I realized I needed to say those things to myself."

I love this story, because it highlights our shared humanity, compassion, but most importantly, it highlights how powerful vulnerability is… and how we can learn so much about our needs and wants from these sacred moments.

Truths to Help Conquer Fear and Vulnerability

- Peoples' opinions about you are only their opinions. Don't make them yours. There is beauty, power, and strength in you, so make these your reality.
- Life is happening for you, not to you. Your Soul is on a quest to know human life, to experience the joys of what this life can offer. By learning the lessons of what the human life can teach, it is not on a quest to play life safe, to be small or to be less than who we are.
- There is a part of you that knows how perfect you are and what you are capable of. It might only be hidden by false stories you have been told, so delete the false stories. Start a new story.
- What exists in the present moment is what it is. It can't change or turn into something. It exists as it is and needs only an awareness of it.
- As much as there is suffering in the world, there are people going through beautiful life-changing moments. Your beautiful moments will come; have faith even if you can't see them now… they are being created behind the scenes.
- It is okay to fail sometimes, and sometimes you will fail. Failures are speed bumps helping you to become more aware and to learn through growth and progress. To have peace in your heart you need to learn to override the thoughts in your mind.
- We can't even begin to imagine how intelligent the Universe would have to be to co-create with us so many moments

of Divine synchronicity. Have faith in the magic of synchronicity to transform your life.

- Nobody has a perfect life. Every person is facing a battle behind closed doors and often a story of heartache you may not even know about. You don't need to compare yourself to others' external life.

- Have faith that the specific situations that are unfolding in your life at the moment serve a higher purpose. Your Soul knows, so trust in its wisdom. Trust plays a huge part in being okay with vulnerability.

- Worrying is consuming and serves no purpose. It has a low vibrational energy. It doesn't stop things from happening; it only serves to make the now harder.

- When you feel emotions, even unpleasant ones, don't try to push them away... Feel them, acknowledge them, and comfort them. Through the acknowledging of emotions, you begin to heal, and you develop the power to move past moments of vulnerability.

- You don't need every part of you to be perfect before you are perfect. Your imperfections combine together to make up YOU, so love all of YOU.

Soul Insights

- In each moment, you are protected by a Universe that is far grander than anything our minds can comprehend. With forces that are too powerful for mere words to describe.

- Change is inevitable. During change have faith that your Soul will bring you courage and specific lessons required for you to spiritually progress. Embrace change and the transformations it brings.

The Energy of Fear

> *"Fear will always subside if you have the courage to release its grips on your heart."*

Fear is something we are all gripped with at least once in our lives, more often than not on a daily basis. Fear is the destroyer of dreams, the creator of doubt and limitations. Fear is the voice in our head that tells us we are small, that our power is limited, and it's the voice that constantly whispers, "Who are you to think you can achieve greatness?" Why does it do this? Because it is afraid that you will recognize greatness is your birthright, and if you remember, this fear loses its attachment to you. So, the voice gets louder the closer you get to live your truth, or doing the right thing.

To face fear head-on we have to acknowledge that the fear exists, not run away from it, as this only causes the fear to grow. It is essential to breakdown fear and work out what the source of the fear is. Often, we can remember a moment in our childhood that created the fear or phobia. Hypnotherapy is a good way to get to the root cause of your fear and heal it at the subconscious level. Stillness can also help to rid fear from your life and bring moments of grace back into your life. Often fear is irrational, and even though we know this, we are unable to shush the voice. If fear has played a large role in your past, in your decision, know that you are not alone in this. Fear, although Soul-crushing is also one of our greatest teachers in courage. Without fear, there would be no need for courage. It serves a very important purpose. The problem is when fear becomes your go-to reaction and when it inhibits you from doing the very thing that sets your Soul alight. Fear is important in an emergency situation, so we still need a healthy dose of it.

Fear has been my number one Soul lesson in this life. This chapter was particularly hard for me to write. If you are a writer, you know the steady stream of commentary you hear in the back of your head. What if you are not good enough? What if you have

life plan that was completely mapped out there would be no room for spiritual growth. We are here to not only develop spiritually but to fully live and embrace a physical existence, vulnerabilities and all. In any given moment, you have choice that will bring you closer to your Soul. Do you choose love? Do you choose kindness? Are you expressing compassion? If so then you are living your purpose. Aligning with these beautiful virtues brings the same back into your life.

As humans, we have a duality life. We know the deepest of love, because we have felt the deepest despairs of pain. As much as we think life sucks, if we really think about it, the way our Soul urges us to, we can understand how truly blessed we are to experience this duality and the lessons they provide for us. If we didn't know what pain is, we wouldn't be able to truly feel love. Hope is the opposite to fear. Hope can bring the cleansing you need to wash away the fear and anxiety. Hope is where the sacred can be found.

There is a part of you that remembers your perfect Divine spark, your true essence of pure love. Sit in stillness, remember, connect, and remove the fear that has been plaguing your heart. Because with a love so grand and ineffable… you have the greatest power of in the Universe always by your side, and you are capable of greatness beyond your comprehension. Release any attachments to the fear of showing up in life raw and authentic. Rise above. Aim for courage instead of perfection. Don't let fear stop you from achieving your greatness. The world needs your light and courage.

Personal Lessons in Courage and Vulnerability

I must admit this chapter was the hardest chapter for me to write. I left it to the last and I almost deleted it after I finished it. This is how consuming fear is in our lives. For months before I cringed whenever I thought about writing the 'Courage' chapter. And if I am to be completely honest, the reason for this is that for me this

Soul lesson is the most difficult, the one I must work hardest at, and doesn't come naturally to me.

I know what to do as I have the knowledge embedded in my Soul, but taking the wisdom to action is a much harder task. I find kindness easy, but vulnerability, courage, and fear make me want to curl up in a ball in my own quiet little corner and silently sing (more like moan) the song *The Sound of Silence*. You know because you are reading this that I eventually pushed through the fear. Because of this, I now have a little extra Soul wisdom that may help to inspire others. Moving outside of my own personal box, solely to inspire, removed my fears, needs, and wants from the equation. I had to be courageous, if not for myself then for others.

When I started my personal spiritual journey, I was sixteen and at a pretty low point in my life, as I felt like I didn't belong. I had reached a point of despair. I stopped eating, not because I wanted to be skinny, but because I didn't see the point anymore. This is when I had my first spiritual breakthrough and Divine grace entered my life. You see, it's these precise moments when you feel like everything is breaking away, crumbling, and you don't know if you can take the pain and hurt anymore that life is working behind the scenes for you. Your breakdown will create an unfolding of events and moments of synchronicity that gain momentum and beautiful Divine breakthroughs.

It hurts my heart to think that most people are only a step away from the incredible breakthrough before they end their life. On my hardest day, I didn't have concrete plans to end my life, but I had lost hope. Talking about this is very raw and I feel so vulnerable but I believe it's important to share these moments with others so we realize we are never alone, there is a Divine presence wrapping us in love every step of our journey, and there is always someone else going through something similar to us. On the breakthrough day, I went to the public library. I was like a zombie, void of emotions and there was a sense of nothingness to me. There was no one else in the library, so I threw my hands in the air and silently said, 'I give up!

If there's something else I need to do on this Earth before I leave please show me!' I sat down on the floor and put my head in my lap, feeling desperate, alone, and scarily at peace.

When I lifted my head, I watched a book fly out from the shelf as if by magic. I picked the book up, trying to make sense of the moment. I looked around to see if anyone else was there, I walked behind the shelf to see if someone had pushed it, but nothing, and no one. I turned the book over in my hand and felt an overwhelming sense of love engulf every single cell in my body. A single tear of overwhelming love and gratitude rolled down my face. The book was called *Mary's Message to The World*, about Virgin Mary apparitions.

As I held the book in my hand, memories started to flood my mind of when I was two years old and I would ask my grandmother to put on a Spanish movie about the Virgin Mary apparition at Fatima instead of cartoons. Instantly I felt loved and needed, where as moments before I had been in the deepest despair. It was a sacred moment fueled with clarity that I was indeed loved and there was still plenty of purpose left in my life.

My life has not been the same since. I asked for help and instantly it was given to me. This is how extraordinary life is. At this present moment we understand very little about the intricate ways the Universe works. What I do know with certainty now is that I am loved, and that every single Soul is loved beyond their wildest dreams. I was reassured with love that I still have purpose. I want you to know that so do you.

Soul-fueled Affirmation: 'I am more powerful and stronger than I give myself credit for. When I hear the voice of fear, where I used to be afraid, I now will endeavor to choose courage.'

Forgiveness

"*A heart that is full of love has allowed the powerful healing transformations that can be found in forgiveness to fill their heart.*"

The Powerful Healing Benefits of Forgiveness

Forgiveness is a Divine virtue, and along with courage it is probably one of the hardest virtues to master. I never said Soul work would be easy, did I? I'm sorry if I led you to believe it would be easy. I promise you, it will be worth it in the end though. We assume love is easy in comparison to forgiveness; kindness is even easier, and gratitude? Well, that is a piece of cake in comparison to forgiveness. What your Soul wants you to realize is that forgiveness is a spiritual act of love, self-love, self-compassion, and kindness. It is all these virtues just gifted with a different wrapping paper.

Our Soul urges us to embrace forgiveness, to increase our spiritual connection, and to obtain happiness in the here and now. Forgiveness is paramount for spiritual progress. Pain and heartache, when held onto for too long, cause etches on our heart that are often hard to repair. Forgiveness fills the holes in the heart with love and kindness putty. It tries to free the heart from blame and hurt. We often think true forgiveness is reserved for the 'spiritually' evolved. But authentic forgiveness is essential for wellbeing and happiness, even for us ordinary folks. It is a virtue that every single Soul is capable of mastering. It is a beautiful act of self-compassion as it softens the heart to allow room for the things that will enrich your Soul. It has the ability to transform trauma into healing, pain into peace, and fear into hope. Forgiveness takes you out of the self and into connectedness.

Forgiveness can aid in unity and brings peace into our lives that we thought wasn't humanly possible before forgiveness existed. Forgiveness helps to remove anger and fears that we often hold onto for far too long. It gives us a much-needed chance at a clean slate. It allows us each to access a deeper level of meaning in love and kindness. In the powerful energy of forgiveness, you realize that you never want another Soul to feel the pain you have felt.

Forgiveness is a personal endeavor; it is a way to release pain in the heart. Forgiveness helps you let go of pain's grip, which can firmly grab hold of your heart. And although you previously may have thought you owned the pain, you no longer need to carry that pain with you. Forgiveness is not about admitting what the other person has done is okay, because in most cases it is not. Forgiveness does not say you agree with the act. We all know what is right and wrong. What forgiveness does is allow you to fill your heart with love to move from a place of pain and distress to one of hope and possible joy and love in the future. Most people do the best they can at their level of consciousness. People in pain, who have lacked love, or have been hurt by someone they love, are more inclined to do the same thing to someone else. It becomes a vicious cycle, which needs to be broken at some point. Each moment of life we are learning what is right, what makes us feel good, and so on. Learning to forgive is one of our greatest blessings. The way that forgiveness graces our life is by unburdening a heart that is too heavy with the pain it has been holding onto from the past. How beautiful would the world be if we could allow more room in our heart for the things that make life complete, such as connectedness, joy, love, and kindness?

We all have a certain amount of the bad stuff that we can store in our hearts and our consciousness. Once it overflows it pours into the spaces reserved for love. Don't let the free spaces be taken up in your heart by pain and anguish. These are the spots where love needs to live. There is no greater joy than seeing someone whose Soul is bruised and battered, who has lost their spark, rise again and have a twinkle hope in their eyes. It is truly beautiful to witness.

Forgiveness Makes You Okay

Forgiveness doesn't make what the other person did to you okay, and often, in acts that require forgiveness, what they did will never be okay. It serves to help the forgiver to heal. By forgiving you are not condoning the act, but you are condemning the act from hardening your heart. At a deep Soul level you are saying to your perpetrator:

'I understand that you are human and you made a mistake. I also recognize that at a Soul level you are love. I can forgive you because I don't need to hold onto this bitterness and pain that has remained in my heart too long. But I am stronger than any pain you have put me through… because my super power is forgiveness.'

If you wish to be a catalyst for kindness, try forgiveness today and bring the happiness and feel-good energy to your life so you can spread your beautiful wings. Holding onto pain creates bitterness. Don't let pain harden your beautiful heart. You are not hard, you are soft. Don't let an act someone else did to you cause you to lose your gentleness. It is not your fault they did that act, and it never was. Everybody makes his or her own choices. It was never your choice to be hurt but it is your choice whether or not you can now learn to be free from that hurt by forgiving. When you hold onto pain or hurt, at a subconscious level you are giving your power over to them. You deserve your power, not them. In an ideal world forgiveness would be easy. This is where the blessing of forgiveness lies, and why if we have the courage to venture into forgiveness we get the chance to watch the miracle of love grace our lives. Use your healing journey into forgiveness for reflecting on an act you would like forgiveness for too. Does it make you feel uncomfortable? Sad? Angry? You deserve forgiveness also. You deserve forgiveness, because everybody makes mistakes, even bad ones. A bad act does and should not define a person. Each day is a brand-new chance to do a bunch of good acts. Use your energy to do good stuff in the world; don't waste your energy on the pain of the past.

Forgiveness is a continual work in progress. One day you will feel powerful, free from attachment, and you will feel 'yep that's it. I've got this in the bag.' And then the next day you will wake up angry, unforgiving, and feeling hurt. Feel these emotions, acknowledge them, the day after, and begin your forgiveness journey again. One day, I assure you, you will be able to look back and wonder when your baby steps turned into big adult strides, and you will be grateful that now your adult strides take no conscious effort anymore. Forgiveness is a process that can take a lifetime to overcome. Keep trying. Keep shining. There is no time limit on releasing the pain from your heart. Welcome the positive effect that change will have in your life, when it is time.

Forgiveness is about changing yourself, not the other person. You can never change someone else; it is their place to implement the changes they require for their life and purpose. You can only ever change yourself. With every breath you take you can begin to consciously choose kindness, and it is kind to forgive. Forgive yourself for your mistakes, forgive everyone that has ever hurt you. Resentment and guilt will cause more harm to you and will manifest as negative emotions such as anger and worry, for you, not them. These emotions will manifest in your energy body first then progress to manifest as physical and psychological disease. Forgiveness also doesn't require the other person to apologize, as it is a personal endeavor, an act of self-kindness... for you. There is no room anymore for anger in your heart, so let it go gracefully.

The Essentials of Forgiveness

- Be present. A heart that is connected to the hurts of the past is missing direct blessings in the **NOW**.

- Release your pain and hurt over to a Divine source, or whatever source you connect to. Connect to your Soul and ask it to give you the strength needed to move to a peaceful state of being.

- At the end of your day, make sure you go over all of the blessings from that day. State the things you were grateful for and remember fondly all the moments of joy and love you experienced. A heart that is connected to these moments struggles to hold onto pain.

- Make a conscious decision every day to choose how you react in undesirable situations. Where you once chose anger, try something different. For example, take three deep breaths in and out before you react. Try to visualize something beautiful that reveals joy in your heart and see if your reactions are less fueled by emotions and more mindful.
- Let go. You have very little control over other people's decisions and choices in life and nor should you want to have control. If they make decisions that you find undesirable, you can't change their decision; you can only choose your own. Let go of what no longer serves you.
- Always choose kindness. When dealing with a situation you only have to ask, 'What is the kindest thing I can possibly do?' It doesn't matter who is right or who is to blame, it only matters who is kind.
- Make sure you apologize if a part you played in the in the incident was less than kind also. This frees your heart from the pain of guilt.
- Love. If you live in the heart space of love, you don't have room for judgments and more love will be attracted to you. Forgiveness is a virtue that when practiced with love is a lot easier.
- Spiritually forgive by trying to move past the physical body and connect with the other person at a Soul level. Remember that there is only oneness and that we are all connected.
- Being kind helps you to learn to forgive, because forgiveness is an act of kindness.

A Pastor's Story of the Power of Forgiveness

A Pastor recently shared a story with me about the powerful benefits forgiveness has had on his life. The story he shared is such a beautiful example of the power of forgiveness and the miracles that unfold when you allow forgiveness to enter you heart that I had to share it with you here. I think the story is even more powerful, because it shows the potential for every single one of us to miss out on blessings when we close our heart.

Years ago, the Pastor lent a good friend of his one thousand dollars. The Pastor had heard his friend needed the money for a computer so he could study and he was going to get a loan that would charge him a very high interest. Not wanting his friend to pay a high interest, the Pastor offered to lend his friend the money as long as he paid it back within a specific timeframe. He didn't want any interest either. This was a lot of money for the Pastor and his young family at the time. Unfortunately, the due date came and went and every time he saw his friend he would give false promises about when he would pay the money back. After each visit with his friend the Pastor started getting more and more resentful. He tried to be kind to his friend, but inside he was hiding his anger. This is when things started to get strange for the Pastor.

During this time, another friend of the Pastor sadly committed suicide. In his will the Pastor was given two thousand dollars and a computer. Even though the Pastor received these gifts he still remained resentful towards his friend about the money he was owed. One day, the Pastor decided to let it go, as he noticed the bitterness and anger was eating him up inside. He decided to let his friend off the hook and told him he no longer needed to pay the money back. The Pastor wanted forgiveness in his heart instead of the anger that was beginning to consume him. He told his friend to consider it as a gift. As soon as he forgave his friend and let him off the hook, he felt he could relax and be around his friend without holding any anger towards him in his heart.

After the act of forgiveness occurred the Pastor found that a phenomenon started to take over his life and people everywhere started to give him computers. It started with the local councilor giving the Pastor's charity ten computers. Then an office building was shutting down and contacted the Pastor about donating a whole office block of computers.

The Pastor runs a fun run to raise funds for his charity and because of this event the local land corporation gave him a thousand dollars and a computer. They were unable to give him a computer as they were out of stock, so they gave him Five Hundred dollars to purchase his own computer. With this money the Pastor was able to buy three computers instead through a government initiative. He gave one of the computers to a bible student of his, and one day the student dropped the computer on the floor and because of this his insurance company paid out two thousand five hundred dollars to the Pastor. With this money he was able to buy even more computers for his church. It was around this time that the Pastor started to notice he was increasingly getting thousand-dollar donations to his church. He even received donations from two family members (who don't attend the same church). Both donated at separate times with a sum of a thousand dollars. To this day the Pastor still gets computers donated to him.

This is such a powerful story that proves how important forgiveness is to open up your heart to the miracles and blessings that are unfolding everyday in your life. Forgiveness helps you to see and receive these blessings, which are available to you always. Imagine how incredible the power of synchronicity was at play here. I am thankful that this kind Pastor shared his story with me, so you can understand what forgiveness in action looks like.

Personal Forgiveness

Out of all the virtues and wisdoms that are included in this book, and even those that aren't in this book, forgiveness may only be required of you a couple of times in your life, unlike the other virtues, which can be infinite in nature. There may be only a couple of times in your life where you will have to be courageous enough to embody the virtue of forgiveness, so you can heal your hurting heart. That is good though, because forgiveness is often hard for us mere mortals to comprehend and to act on. One act of pain, hurt or malice may take an entire lifetime to forgive. Don't wait too long though. Start the process now, remembering each conscious step you take is one step towards healing, and that often for every step forward, you might take two steps backwards, and that is okay.

When I think about my life, I would say I have been pretty blessed. There have been people along the way, whom I have had to forgive, but often the pain they caused was minor and the challenge wasn't so complex. There has been one person I have learnt to forgive and I am grateful I allowed the forgiveness to enter to my heart, because the love I felt afterwards can only be described as bliss. When that moment of blissful peace entered my heart I wondered why I ever used that space in my heart for hurt and pain before. The person I needed to forgive was my Dad. Often the people we need to forgive are those closest to us, because it is easy for us to accept how a stranger can hurt us, but someone we love? How can we even begin to comprehend that?

Our story is a complex one, but when I look back I can honestly say the love moments far outshone the hurt. On quiet reflection, I also realized I wasn't the only victim; my Dad was also the victim, and in certain moments I could have chosen a kinder option. I still love my Dad unconditionally and I now accept his decisions are nothing to do with me and I cannot judge. But because I chose self-kindness our energies have gone separate ways… for now. I can't say what the future will hold, but I do know with all my heart I chose the kindest option there was at the time. I have so much gratitude for my Dad. He was and is my greatest teacher and his love for me as a child was truly palpable. Where hurt and pain used to reside, now love does. The reason I was angry with him, but mostly hurt, is because the choices he made excluded me from his life. Who am I to judge his choices? I now know it is not my place anymore.

I had been holding on to the pain and the hurt because they

fed my need. But along the way I learnt to separate the Soul from the man. I needed to remember his essence. So instead of trying to fix him, I learnt to forgive him. In the process, I learnt to forgive myself too. I did the best I could have done with my level of consciousness at the time.

Forgiveness reigns where pain and hurt once co-existed. I am kind to him now through prayer, positive thoughts, forgiveness, and random acts of kindness for which he knows nothing about. I believe I chose him as my father at a deep Soul level for the lessons in forgiveness and kindness he would teach me. I feel he has done a fantastic job in teaching me the lessons my Soul chose to learn in this lifetime, and for that I am truly grateful. The day I chose to connect to the very heart of his Soul, instead of the man, I had peace. I feel immense gratitude for my father and the role he played in my continued evolution, and in doing that I still always honor the pain and hurt I felt.

Forgiveness Exercise

It is often hard to find the courage to say the words we need to say to our loved ones in order to heal and move on. We can learn to forgive but speaking the words feels too raw. To allow forgiveness to impact your heart, a good way to do this is to write a letter to the person you need to forgive. It is important to recognize their Soul; the part of them that is free from anger, that would never hurt you, and that is perfect and whole.

There is a part of you that wants to forgive. The same part of you that made you love them in the first place… The letter is not a place to vent your anger. It is also not a place to throw hurtful comments. The letter is a place where you can be free to express your deepest Soul's yearnings for forgiveness. It is a place to recognize the essence of the Soul you are angry at. It is a place to love. Even if the thought of sending the letter is too impossible to comprehend, still write the letter… It sends the intention to the Universe that you forgive or at least you want to learn to. It releases you from the pain and anger that has heavily weighed your heart down.

Below is an example of a letter I have written to my Dad. I wrote it a couple of years ago and never showed a soul (until now). Although I didn't personally show my Dad, I energetically sent it to him from my heart to his. I released it into the cosmos to do its healing work. And hopefully at a spiritual level it can relieve him of any pain and suffering he may be feeling. On several occasions I have verbalized the sentiments within this letter to him, but for whatever reasons, they were not received. The letter is my conscious decision to let go of the hurt and the pain that does not serve ME anymore. It is a chance for me to honor the Soul of the man I love so dearly

I have learnt it is not my place to heal him. I have gone on my own healing journey and I now recognize that healing is very personal. The person must want to heal. The person must be willing to open up their heart and pour the contents out with so much vulnerability it hurts. The person must be willing to admit that maybe they have played a much larger role in the unfolding of their life than they would like to imagine. That is often the hardest thing we will have to do. It is easy to blame someone else; it is much harder to own some of that responsibility.

The wisdom of my Soul reminds me that at his core, my Dad is nothing but love. I see this when I look into his eyes. It is not easy to witness a body that is so pained. But love is always easy. There is nothing he could do or has done that will make me love him any less. I have seen his greatness in his heart, I know it exists, and therefore I forgive. Forgiveness and compassion now reside in my heart, in the spot that is no longer reserved for anger and sadness. Who do you need to forgive? Remember, when writing the letter, a true spiritual practice is to align with the heart of your Soul, and to bless them and genuinely wish them joy and happiness. This will open up your heart space for personal happiness.

Example of Forgiveness Letter

Dear Dad,

I hope that you know love in this moment; I hope that the pain in your heart is filled with a Divine love so grand that your heart explodes with pure joy. May grace touch every corner of your world and leave you feeling whole and loved again. I look forward to one day being able to embrace you with the deepest love and to say thank you, for your love, lessons in forgiveness, and courage. I am sorry for any pain I have caused you, for any love that you have not been able to receive and that I haven't been able to express to you, but I know it is there. And know this... you are an amazing soul, whose wisdom and joy has been lost to a world so filled with pain and heartache, but I am certain one-day it will be found. You have been my greatest teacher and I will forever hold you in my thoughts and prayers. I forgive you Dad, and I have nothing but love for you. And even though I was hurt in the past by your words or decisions, I recognize that we all make mistakes, as we are all human. Wishing you peace in your mind and a palpable love in your heart.

I love you, Dad.

Namaste Kylie x

There is no greater freedom to want the best for people, especially those who have hurt you.

Self-Forgiveness

Over the years, I have learned to hold deep gratitude for the mistakes I have made in my life (weirdo, I know) but the mistakes I have made have led to plenty of opportunities for my Soul to learn and grow. It is all about progress, evolving... growing into love. Every day you wake up you have been blessed with a fresh day ahead, a new canvas to paint on, and a new chapter to write about. It is a chance for you to grace your life with the powerful healing benefits of self-forgiveness, in the process teaching you to love.

Start right now though, as tomorrow is not promised, and you don't need to waste one more single breath on wishing you could have done better in the past. You don't need to hold onto regrets. Forgive all of you. Be kind to yourself, as when you are kind to yourself your kindness to others expands. It is hard to forgive others if you struggle to forgive yourself. Forgive yourself for your mistakes, forgive everyone who has ever hurt you, and let it go gracefully.

I'm going to spill some truth here. You are going to continue to make mistakes every day and you will hurt people, but at the end of the day, you are human. Forgive yourself for your future mistakes, as guilt will cause more harm to you and will manifest as negative emotions such as anger and worry. Embrace forgiveness, self-compassion, and self-kindness wholeheartedly. Forgiveness is the icing on the cake when it comes to personal transformation and spiritual development, especially if you want to light the candle to your heart.

In this life, you are a human being trying to develop spiritually, trying to make the most out of this life and all of its sublime beauty. You are also in the beginning stages of trying to master the skill of hurdling by learning to jump over some bad shit along the way. Rest assured that your Soul is in the process of evolving. This moment will be the last moment you will experience this life under these circumstances with the wonderful people you have in it. Yesterday is the past and the future can change in a blink of an eye. You will make tons of mistakes and you will hurt people, but afterwards you have to learn to forgive yourself. A mind that is caught in the stories of the past is missing out on the moments of bliss and grace in the present. In this moment, you are free... but only until you give energy to the pain and guilt that is stored in your heart. Your Soul wants you to know that if you have the courage to move past the stories that you hold onto and forgive yourself, you will see the ultimate truth of you, which is love.

> ***Soul-fueled Affirmation: 'Today, I will let myself off the hook. I now recognize that I did the best I could have done at the time with the level of consciousness I had at the time, and I recognize that even if I could have done better there is no turning back the clock, but tomorrow I will choose to do better... because now I know better.'***

8

HAPPINESS & AUTHENTICITY

"You are entitled to unlimited happiness and potential. There is no quota that says you have had too much. Know that you always deserve authentic happiness, today and always."

Happiness

> *"Joy is how the Universe pours its beauty through you*
> *so others get to glimpse this Divine beauty, and for a*
> *moment experience Divine bliss. Be a channel for this*
> *Divine joy."*

Authentic happiness is the kind of happiness that makes your eyes smile. We all know people like this who seem to smile from their Soul. Often, these people whom despite adversity and having little materialistically, still have an undeniable twinkle in their eyes. It is captivating to be in the presence of one of these souls, and as it fills our heart with pure joy being in their presence… it also leaves us with a snippet of hope that our own lives will be blessed with the same authentic joy. This spark of authentic happiness is available to us all. There is enough happiness to go around for everyone. Your Soul wants you to know that authentic happiness is always a by-product of living all of the Soul lessons and virtues presented in this book. Living a virtuous life for the Soul purpose of inspiring and bringing love to the world is the secret to happiness we have all been searching for.

We have all been lucky enough to have moments of happiness in our lives, but often this happiness is fleeting, especially if it is obtained through achievements and success. When these moments of happiness start to wane, we get fearful and create a new benchmark for ourselves for success, because we are afraid this will be the only way we can be happy. We are afraid that by being ordinary or by living in the moment, we will lack what we need to be happy. Each moment of our lives is a chance to be happy, with what is, as it is.

True happiness, the authentic kind, requires altruism, courage, and forgiveness, and is cultivated only through practice and effort. Your Soul beams with joy each time you show kindness, express love or offer forgiveness, and this joy lasts for an eternity. Living an ordinary life through tender love, kindness, altruism, spirituality, and persistent effort will evolve into an extraordinary happy life. The extraordinary in life is experienced when you get to perform pure acts of love. Practicing virtues is a conscious way we use to awaken our Soul essence, thus linking us to authentic happiness in the here and now.

The Happiness Trap

We are led to believe through media and other sources that we need to look externally for our happiness, through things such as a new house, a car, makeup, and miracle wrinkle cream. And because there is no money to be made for living a virtuous life... it is not as popular as it should be. Because the truth is, true happiness can only be found when you live a conscious life from the heart, through altruism, acceptance, and love. There are no short cuts to authentic happiness, and there is definitely no way to buy your happiness.

You can start by beginning to look into the heart of one another and connecting at a Soul level. It's hard not to love, or be kind or be compassionate when you connect to the very heart of another Soul. When we connect we begin the process to being able to remove war, poverty, and racism from our world. The snowball effect from each person who includes living kindness in his or her lives is phenomenal. If the world is unhappy, how can we truly have authentic personal happiness?

Now more than ever, the world needs to evolve. For evolution to occur, kindness must be present. Love must be our guiding grace and compassion must reign. The world is in a sad state of affairs. Maybe not worse than other times in history but still enough where we all feel this low level of anxiety, pressure, and fear. Living in these spaces unfortunately doesn't allow for our Soul to connect with us to help enrich our lives and those that our lives get to touch. When we live with humility, a grateful heart, when we promote kindness, compassion, and love, we get to experience authentic happiness. It is the repercussion of living these virtues. We can begin to be the catalyst for change we wish to see in world one person, and one act of kindness at a time. Not only for personal happiness, but so others get to be blessed with the same opportunities for joy and light that we so desire.

Happiness is something that must be worked on daily. It gets easier with practice but there is no magical external ingredient that will bring you the peace and happiness your heart desires. Life doesn't work like this. Happiness is always a work in progress, and no matter how hard we try to avoid it, we are always going to have to face hard times. Even if everything in our life is perfect, we still won't be happy unless we are internally happy. We must stop searching externally, or at things or achievements to sustain or obtain happiness. Happiness needs a conscious effort, a willingness to be mindful of our thoughts and to help others to obtain authentic happiness, for us to be authentically happy. To some degree, we do have control over our happiness, and ultimately happiness is a choice, but without inner peace we can't be authentically happy.

Soul Wisdom for Authentic Happiness

- Incorporating kindness and other virtues into daily life will increase your happiness and a sense of wellbeing. Try it today. Do one act of kindness after you put this book down, no matter how small, and then watch what happens to your life. Blessings will occur quicker than you can count. I can guarantee that even just one act of kindness will bring an abundance of what I call "Soul happiness" to your life.
- Smile: The smile is the language of the Soul. When you smile you enter into a contract with love. A smile gifts someone with hope and aids in unity.
- Regardless of your beliefs, or what religion you follow, universally we can almost all agree that laughter is the best

medicine. Do something that makes you deep belly laugh today. It feels good to laugh. During the moment of laughter all your problems are forgotten and you connect with the universal energy of joy. A moment of laughter is a sacred moment; there is a brief moment when you feel you might even cry because the joy will connect you to your source.

- In our constant pursuit of 'busyness' we have forgotten the sacred art of being. In every moment, we are gifted with so much that will bring our life pure happiness: a smile from a child, the love from a friend, or the kindness from a stranger. Sometimes we can get so caught up in the busyness of life that we often forget to look at the gifts we have in each and every moment. Joy lies in the simplicity and perfection of each moment. There is nothing else needed to be joyful but to live in the present moment.

- Make the choice to try to live and breathe happiness. Each day when you wake up choose to express gratitude for this glorious life. It is not always easy but it is worth it.

- If you could see yourself the way you truly are, without the stories you have been told about who and what you are, you would cry tears of joy with the beauty of you. Try to see yourself today through your Soul eyes. Don't believe any of the stories you have been told that tell you, you are anything less than perfect.

- Always do your best. Your best is always good enough. Some days your best is better than other days. Be okay with this.

- Your thoughts belong to you. Your thoughts are extremely powerful, because they are the one place where you have complete control. Release thoughts that diminish your power and that stop you experiencing the happiness you so rightly deserve. Don't listen to a negative thought. Just notice it come and go. The only language the Soul speaks is love.

- Exquisite joy is felt when you shine your light on others for the pure intention of making them happy, just because you want to see them smile. When your intention to bring joy to another Soul is pure, you can be certain that your life will be blessed with the same exquisite joy.

- Often people get scared when they have been happy for a while. Like something bad is brewing on the horizon. Your Soul wants you to know that there is absolutely no quota that says you have had too much happiness. Know that you are entitled to a well of infinite happiness always. The Universe that loves you unconditionally is always on your side, trying to help point your life in the right direction, that of happiness.

Steps to Being Authentically Happy

- Step One: Learn to savor every Divine morsel of happiness and joy that you experience. Really embrace these moments. Look for them. Feel immense gratitude for them. Honor them but don't be afraid to move on and welcome the chance for another moment of joy to grace your life.
- Step Two: Be authentic. You only ever need to be you. When you try to change yourself to fit a mold or you look for outside validation, you slowly give your power for happiness away. If everyone is wearing brown and your favorite color is pink… wear pink… Even if every single person is looking at you, you know you won't be happy wearing brown.
- Step Three: Let things go that no longer brighten your spark. Let what happened in the past stay there. It serves no purpose for the now.
- Step Four: Look at everyone and everything with eyes of love… right down to the cereal that floats around your breakfast bowl in the morning. Why? Because you didn't need to harvest the oats, wheat, and corn yourself. It's the simple things in life that bring us the most joy.

- Step Five: Always Be kind. Genuinely happy people are happy because they want to see other people equally as happy.
- Step Six: Always follow the calling of your Soul and listen to her wisdom. Be courageous enough to follow her as she leads you in the direction of happiness. Don't question the path to happiness. Have trust that the path you are on will lead you to happiness.

Shining My Light On Happiness

"Life is filled with so much potential for joy and undeniable magic. Be willing to see the miracles of joy… they will be presented to you often if you are open to her blessings."

When I began to listen to the calling of my Soul to live and breathe kindness, I started to see the simplicity in happiness, and before long it became simply a part of life. By working on the other Soul lessons you can be sure authentic happiness will grace your life more and more.

Bad things will happen, sometimes even terrible things; I'm not naïve and I don't wish to sugarcoat the hardships of life. Today, choose happiness and gratitude instead of negativity, compassion instead of judgment, kindness instead of selfishness. These virtuous acts will always help make your life a little brighter, and the lives of those your light touches. It's hard not to be filled with joy in such moments.

A person grows by following the drive inside of them, by learning to release any fear stopping them from shining their light on Earth, even when it is easier to walk away. I'm sure Mother Teresa's job was not easy. The world is a much better place because she shined her light. We have a responsibility in life to not only ourselves, or family but to the collective consciousness of our planet. When I began to look at it in this way, I began to understand that choosing happiness takes on a bigger importance. Make the choice today to be happy or not to be happy. The law of manifestation says that what you believe, feel, and think you will attract into your life. So, if you choose to be happy, the Universe will give you more things to be happy about.

We are a work in progress. Like an artist develops their skills, so do we humans. For one moment, let your imagination soar, and imagine being completely happy. Imagine being the next version of Oprah. Why not? The limit is higher than the sky. Often, we get caught up in our own needs and wants, but the truth is, the world also needs your light, so please shine it as bright as you can even if others are blinded by it. It is a lot of effort to choose to be happy frequently; but eventually it becomes second nature.

You will spend times in bad spaces, and that's okay, but don't give up. Dig yourself out, whether via natural remedies, exercise, diet changes, supports groups, prayer meditation, it doesn't matter. What does matter is that you keep trying. We all form a piece of the collective puzzle. Without your puzzle piece, there is an important piece missing from us all. Joy is a gift from the Universe so embrace it and remember life is sublimely glorious. Forget about the bad day you had yesterday. Tomorrow is a brand new day, and a new page in your book. How will your story continue? Make it a happy one.

The happiest of hearts are the ones that can laugh at themselves, embrace their own flaws, and make these flaws their future strengths. As much as we think happiness is difficult to obtain, the truth is, as humans we make things more difficult then they truly are. The answer to most of life's questions and problems is pretty simple: living and breathing kindness, compassion and love. There is a reason that there is a link between altruism and personal happiness; it's because the more engaged and giving you are, the happier you make other people, and the brighter your Soul smiles.

Authenticity

Putting Authenticity into Action

> *"Your job is to show up to life raw and authentic, and watch as the Universe works its synchronistic magic through you."*

In any given moment, you have a chance to shine your light on Earth so bright that you leave a trail of sparkly love wherever you tread. To leave the biggest footprint and to get the optimal brightness out of your light you need to follow your authentic voice. What is it that makes your heart sing? Do that! Actually... do lots of that! Authentic living enables you to be true to your heart, and follow the calling of your Soul.

The first step in the process is to show up and commit. It doesn't sound very complex but often it is the hardest step. All of the other steps are easier if you commit to the first step. The second step on the path to true authentic living requires deep reflective processing. It requires asking the questions you may not want answers for. To live authentically requires accessing the deep hidden well of talents and desires that may have been lying dormant for years. The third step requires you to swim through the depth of vulnerability, and often it requires immense courage to move past the fear of ridicule or failure and to take the big first step into unknown territory. Know that if you are following your authentic spark, you will always be successful.

Authentic living is not about being nice and it's not necessarily easy. Authentic living is about creating a passion-filled life that gives you the permission to live the way you truly want. Here's the truth: you don't need permission, and you never have. Who are you seeking permission from? If you have a calling in your heart, right there is where you can find the permission slip that you need. You just need to follow the messages of your heart, and then watch how fulfilling your life becomes. The fear will always subside.

People living authentically, radiate happiness and joy. Can you imagine what it would feel like if every single day you got to be the authentic version of you? You will get to dazzle everyone your light gets to touch with your brightness. The game-changers in the world live authentically, and are brave enough to push the boundaries of what is considered 'normal.' Remember, what is considered normal today will seem archaic to future generations. All because some brave soul had the courage to live their passion and move past the fear of failure. There is a part of you that knows how perfect you are and what you are capable of. Your greatness is probably only hidden by false stories you have been told about your apparent imperfections or your perceived failures. Often, what we think is failures are moments where the Universe is creating unseen magic behind the scenes for you.

Ways to Live Authentically

- Become aware of what ignites feelings of passion and happiness
- Be open to feeling a genuine sense of wellbeing and happiness
- Be prepared to open the floodgates to the fear/failure presenting itself in you. Find the courage to move past the fear
- Live a virtuous life with compassion, kindness, and courage
- Follow through and be committed to living your authentic life
- Fall in love with yourself, just the way you are.
- Find ways to learn who the real you is and try to remove yourself from all of the roles that you play in life. Use your intuition to find out who you truly are so you know what dreams to follow.
- Try to detach from other people's judgments of you
- Realize that other people's judgments are just that… their judgments, and they have nothing to do with you.

Imagine

Imagine how relationships would flourish if there was only ever authenticity from the beginning, if you didn't have to change the person 'you are' to the person you should be. The sacred can be found in you, so you do not need to search outside of yourself. Everything you have ever needed can always be found inside of you.

Imagine… a life that is authentic, a life that you were able to live on purpose, with purpose!

Never in history has there been such a big platform to follow your own authentic voice. I can't stress the point enough… Anything that is worth it is never easy initially but eventually it will become effortless because you are following the call of your Soul. If it makes you happy, then do it. Don't let other people tell you that you can't. Don't wait. Life flies by in a blink of an eye and at the end of life we often have regrets. Don't let being true to your authentic self be your regret. Being different means that you are doing the right thing; you are being your authentic self and a voice for others who are also different. If you can't do it for yourself, then do it for others, to provide them with the inspiration to live with authenticity. Your bravery might give them the courage they need.

Live your life on purpose… stop waiting for things to fall into place. They may never fall into place. You may need to take big steps towards following the call of your Soul. Make your 'Soul' purpose in life to live with authenticity. The truth is, you were created for greatness, happiness, and joy, even if you have temporarily forgotten it. Go and do just that. Search internally for the courage I know is inside of you to be free to live your authentic life. When you achieve this self-acceptance through your courage you will find the little niche in the world where you will truly belong. This can only lead to one road… authentic happiness.

The life we often live is a safe life, so we can fit inside a box, which says we are 'normal.' Life is not about being safe. Contrary to popular belief, nobody in the box is happy. Even it appears externally that they are, they are not, unless the box is them living authentically. Every single soul you know is facing a battle, often hidden by a brave face. Most people have a story of heartache you know nothing about. If only we were brave enough to admit our failures so we never had to feel alone. Because the truth is, we are never alone in our battles. There is always someone along the way facing a similar battle. Don't let the fear of failure stop you from achieving your greatness. The world needs your individual light and courage.

Often, we don't live our authentic path because we fear change. Change is not something we should fear; change allows for the unfolding of our Soul to shine through in all we do. Life is a process of constant change. Change can bring the cleansing that your Soul has been seeking to progress forward on your unique spiritual journey. Try to embrace change and transformations…. This will help make your life journey far smoother after you get over the initial speed humps, which always seem more daunting then they truly are.

Purpose Driven Authenticity

When you wake up in the morning, what do you think about? If you work behind the counter at retail shop but your thoughts are consumed with singing, you are a singer, or at least you are at this phase of your life. Each day of your life do something that makes your Soul burst with joy and fills your life with purpose and meaning. Even if you don't get paid for the thing you love, still make time every day to do it. Be okay if you fall down and get right back up to try again.

Our western culture has gotten to the point that working and paying the bills is the most important part of life, so in the end we pretty much just exist. What is the point of just existing? It is obviously not making us happy. Is the fear of survival inhibiting your ability to live authentically, to follow the calling of your Soul? Our purpose and passion varies in depth and constantly evolves over the course of our life. Being human calls us to bring forth our authenticity to allow our Soul mission to shine through in all that we do.

Bronnie Ware, in her beautiful book *Five Regrets of the Dying* pointed out that over and over again in her time in palliative care she found that one of the biggest regrets most people have on their death bed is that they worked too much and they wished they had made more time in their life to do the things that made their heart leap with joy. Don't let living an inauthentic life be your regret. It doesn't matter how old you are, you are still capable of being authentic and listening to the call of your Soul. We are beautiful wise beings and our Soul knows time as endless. Don't let something like age stop you from living, dreaming, and believing.

Please know that I'm not encouraging you to go and quit your job right now. I live in this world and I'm fully aware that certain things take time, and that patience is also necessary to hone your skills until the Universe is ready to release your complete awesomeness onto a world that is ready for your authentic Soul spark.

Keep in mind that you can have a job that pays your bills while you still do a job that sets your Soul on fire... the first one is just a means to manifest the second one. Work every day at whatever sparks your light and then, one day, you will find your calling has perfectly aligned to suit you and you will finally get paid for what you love. Nobody becomes an instant success. Usually, years of hard work finally lead to 'success.' If you love it, do it. Success lies in you following your authentic spark, and after that everything else just falls into place.

I believe in you, your Soul believes in you, the Universe supports you, but most importantly, do you believe in you? If you are feeling stuck, sad or unfulfilled look inside of yourself and see if you are being authentic to your higher calling. Let the wings of faith carry you to your next destination on your journey to authenticity.

Soul-fueled Affirmation: "I am so beautiful! My Soul shines so bright every time I smile, laugh or spread joy. Today, I will take a moment to smile, to breathe, to live in pure joy, so others can see the authentic me."

Following the Call of My Soul

Over the last couple of years I have learnt to pick up and really listen to the call from my Soul, and with it I have come to a certain place of peace. A place where I am free to be myself, a place free from fears. In my authentic place I no longer care what opinions or judgments others have of me. And when they do have judgments, I have slowly begun to accept that they are just that – other people's judgments. I don't need to form an attachment to them; it really is about them not me.

I no longer live in the drama of seeking outside validation or approval anymore. I no longer let fear control my every move, which is something I was unconsciously doing. I began to realize that the decisions I was making out of fear were only inhibiting my endless possibilities for happiness and peace.

I now choose to live with Authenticity and because of this I no longer need to change the person I am into a person that everyone else thinks I should be. I am only being myself. There is so much freedom that comes from this… and with freedom comes peace and joy.

When I first began to tear back the layers I had unconsciously created through the years, I began by getting rid of the stuff that longer served my Soul, the stuff that dimmed my sparkle, that others had assured me was necessary for me to shine. After all the layers were removed it felt like a weight had been lifted off my shoulders and for the first time in my life I knew what it felt like to be authentically me.

Because once all of the layers disappear all that you are left with is simplicity and love. It didn't take me long to realize that this is the only place where I feel home, where I felt a palpable peace. The longer I spend in this space, the kinder I become and the more I unfold into who I was always suppose to be, me, fun, weird, childish, definitely cant fit in a box, deeply spiritual and full of love… Kylie.

How do you Know You are Following the Call?

The first thing I think about when I wake up, besides being grateful for a brand-new day, is writing. When I write, I feel alive. I feel joy. I feel inspired. I feel connected to my Soul. The truth is, up until this point, my writing has not paid my bills. Each day, when I wake up, I know I need to make some time for writing. I try to write every moment I can, in the few spare moments I have in my busy days raising and loving my kids. I write in the toilet on my phone, I write when the kids are in bed, even though I really want to watch a new series on Netflix, because I know that if I don't write I will feel like there is a piece of me missing.

And even though it is hard to write on top of everything else I need to do, what inspires me is the thought that one day my writing might have the ability to help someone through a tough time. If I don't write I would be purposely avoiding the call of my Soul, because I have picked up her call and we all know there is no hanging up once you have answered. No matter how many times you might want to. Wanting to help make the world a better place is often inspired from a Soul-fueled purpose. Everyone asks me what my real job is when I tell him or her I am writer. At present, my real job is writing, but I pay some of my bills by being a teacher aide. Because, the truth is, we live in a world where we need money.

I started simply by writing micro blogs on Twitter, and then eventually my personal blog, and then I was asked to write the occasional article or guest blog. And now, finally, I wrote the book you are holding in your hand. This process took years, and often when I thought about giving up, the Universe would send me a beautiful sign that I was doing the right thing. These moments of synchronicity only fueled the desire I had to not quit and to continue to follow the calling of my Soul to see where she might take me, to show up, even though I wanted to hide.

You will never go without if you follow the calling of your Soul, as the Universe will always provide for you, even if it is a casual job at a fast food restaurant. It is still a way to support your authenticity, so don't knock it back if it gives you the ability to have authentic happiness. I have a wise cousin-in-law, Kane, who is brave enough to live life fiercely every day with pure authenticity. There is no one like Kane; he has a unique gift with creating one-of-a- kind art pieces out of recycled metal. And although Kane often finds it hard to pay his bills, he is living off the grid, doing the very thing that makes his Soul sing, and he inspires others everyday by living his dream and following his own authentic spark. When I feel like giving up I say to myself, what would Kane tell you to do? I know instantly that he would tell me to do the thing that sets your Soul on fire every day. Okay Kane, I will. Because I see what happiness you have achieved by living your life on purpose in your own unique way, I know this is the road to authentic happiness.

One day, you will find that your 'hobby' will pay the bills… or at the very least feed the part of your Soul that won't be happy until you live your dream. Always say YES to the call of your Soul. Your calling will always align with love, will be joy-infused, and will help to bring peace or joy to Earth. We were given the best gift of all our own uniqueness. No one in the Universe has your beautiful Soul, your unique blueprint, and your light. Don't waste it. Use it.

Finding Your Life Purpose Exercise (Allow 20-30 Minutes)

What you will need for this exercise: A pen and paper, and a quiet place to sit.

1. Sit in a quiet spot somewhere. If meditation is something you enjoy, sit quietly in meditation for at least ten minutes, focusing on your breathing. If you don't feel comfortable meditating for the next ten minutes try to become aware of your surroundings. Notice the trees, listen for the sounds of the birds, and notice how the sun feels on your skin.

2. Grab your pen and paper and write down all the things that make your heart sing; anything that makes you feel all warm and fuzzy inside. Do you adore animals or enjoy painting? Try to connect to your inner self, try to remember what you loved as a child, and look beyond the person that you project to the world. If you connect with a Divine being ask them for assistance in giving you images in your mind's eye of the things that will bring you happiness. Make sure you write everything down, whether you hear it, imagine it, and vibrantly see it in your mind's eye. Write all the things you see, hear, and feel.

3. Look at what you have written down – clump the things together that seem to have a common thread – and see if you notice a hint at what your life purpose might be.

4. Take the first step - if you love to write, start a blog. Post more frequently to social media. But start somewhere and don't give up. Before long, you will have a book. You don't even need to think about the next step, just focus on the first step, and the second step will always come to you.

5. Never give up. Keep trying and shining. You will be thankful you did in the end.

6. Remember to do something little every day in the direction of your life purpose. It may be hard work but eventually life will flow. The world needs your light.

You are beautiful as you are
You are complete as you are
You are loved as you are

At the end of the day...

Conclusion

"In the end, the only thing that matters is that you loved. Everything else is just the icing on the cake. And remember, if all you did was love today, that's enough, and it will always be enough."

The Simplicity of Soul Wisdom

When we learn to connect to the essence of our Soul, we align with the universal wisdom that has always been inside of us, which has a wealth of knowledge and love to share with us if we are open to seeing and hearing its blessings. We have all been gifted with this wisdom. It is often just hidden so deep down that we no longer know how to access it. The wisdom is not foreign, and contrary to popular opinion, you don't have be someone who is spirituality 'special' to live and breathe this wisdom. We all know the simple lessons of love, kindness, forgiveness, and gratitude, but often we forget to live these Soul-inspired virtues, which are how we humans connect to our Soul, the Universe, and to every other human being.

We are continuously told from the media, advertising, and manufacturers what will bring us happiness. We are encouraged to fear others who are different, or to hate particular people because they may change our way of life. We are even encouraged to purchase particular products because we need that item to bring something to our life that we are led to believe we are lacking. I believe that all media is fake. The truth is, we are all in this together and the stories of separation that the media spreads only increases our fear and our survival instinct, which unfortunately leaves very little room to be truly virtuous.

We can no longer sit passively on the sidelines anymore and wait for those that are in power to change the world; we must be courageous enough to take a stand, to be the social activist we admire, not only using prayer and meditation as our method of fixing stuff. We must be brave enough to venture where no man has gone and be willing to get our hands dirty in the process. This can only be achieved by living the spiritual virtues of courage, forgiveness, kindness, and compassion. Living and breathing these virtues will undoubtedly bring you the most exquisite joy you could ever imagine, and with it, an instant knowing of which road you need to take that will lead you to your own personal Soul purpose. You can be certain that the road will always include love.

The beauty of your Soul wisdom and what most of the media and organizations don't want you to know is, it is free. There is no money to be made in the Soul business. At this point in time we all know money can't buy happiness anyway. Living and breathing the virtues of gratitude, forgiveness, and compassion can help you obtain personal happiness; but beyond that, it is the only way we change the world. Your Soul is an ineffable ball of love, so pure, so full of light that the beauty of it is indescribable. That is you, as you are not separate from this. It is the same love at the heart of every single Soul that you come in contact with too, and if they don't externally represent this, it is merely that they have forgotten their brilliance. Please help them to remember to see their brilliance by reflecting your own light on them. Be the change we so desperately need to see in the world.

You can be the Catalyst for Change the World Needs

By actively engaging and living kindness and other acts of love we have the innate ability to change the story that has already been told, a million times before, the same throughout all of human history, but differently. In the past, we humans haven't painted a very pretty picture. We have the ability to change what picture we paint in the future. Never before in history have we had so many opportunities to make an impact and consequently change humanity's future story. This is why I wrote this book at this time. A world that is built on altruism with authentic acts of compassion and love is the story we have all been yearning to read, to write, and to live. A world filled with the virtues of gentleness, joyfulness, unity, and peacefulness is a beautiful world and one, together we deserve to live in.

We need to stop looking at these concepts as utopian and out of reach; peace is accessible, it may not be easy, it may take hard work, but if we individually partake in our own authentic way of living, we consciously aid in developing a world we want our children to grow up in. I for one know that I am not okay with the way the world is today. If there is any chance I can change the trajectory of human evolution, I will. I am a huge believer that one person can impact the world and make a huge difference. What if that person is you? **IT IS YOU**… And it is also me – together we can do this. I no longer want to make up excuses about how bad the world is as the excuses are the problem. The solution is becoming a catalyst for the change I want to see. It is my hope that the future generations will look back on our time and see game-changers. They will be reminded that this time in history was the moment that light was brought to Earth, and they will look at us as brave souls who even in the face of immense adversity, individually and collectively we continued to rise and shine.

Collectively, we have so much growing to do and so much fixing before we reach our innate abilities for selfless kindness and complete unity. But please know that we as humans have an immense capacity for love, compassion, and kindness; we are wired for this, so unity is not beyond us, we have just been afraid for far too long. I'm not naïve to the fact that we currently live in a world that is filled with greed, fear, malice, and selfishness, and often it becomes so overwhelming that it is easier to become apathetic and to turn away from all of the pain. We need people who are courageous enough to not take the easy path.

The world needs us individually to choose courage over comfort, choose to conquer fear instead of playing it safe, and to always choose love instead of simply existing, because without the brave few who will choose connectedness over apathy, the world will stay the same. I believe in you. I believe your Soul is guiding you to be the change maker that we need in the world. We are the bringers of peace that we have been hoping for; we are the ones that will bring the love the world so desperately needs to heal. We can do it. You can do it. Know you are not in this alone… I will join you. We can all do our part in achieving global peace by acting from our own heart center in everything we do. We have the ability to leave this

Earth a better place because we were here, because we were kind, because we loved.

> **Soul-fueled Affirmation:** *"I now choose to see the good that is all around me in the world, and I now choose to be the good I want to see in the world."*

The Beautiful Journey into Love

I hope that through this journey of learning and trying to incorporate the wisdom your Soul wants you to access, you are now starting to remember the keys to your personal authentic happiness. You can have the personal happiness and transformations you seek by following, practicing, and living all of the virtues and wisdoms contained within this book, right here and now, regardless of the hardships or adversities you are having at the moment or you have previously faced in the past. They aren't really profound, but trust me, they work. And even if you only gained one insight or felt one moment of clarity, or a yearning to connect to your Soul, or you only align with one virtue, this book has served its purpose. The purpose of it is for you to continually grow, learn, inspire, and, of course, to love.

Your soul wisdom is like a fountain; it will continually pour new sources of inspiration into your heart, if you let it, everyday there is something new to learn, and a new chance to love. This wisdom is constantly available to you, and just when you think you have it all figured out, a new wave of clarity and insight will wash over you and pour even more love into your heart. Your Soul essence is not separate from you, and it is available to you always. Show it gratitude, to align with its wisdom, and express love to make it shine through you. By listening to the call of your Soul to live and to be a catalyst for change and peace, your light will begin to shine at its brightest.

It is easy to get caught up in the complexities of life, and it is helpful to remember that life is not about perfection and it is not about living only for personal gain. It is about recognizing that personal authentic happiness can be gained only when we help others, by gifting our heart and Soul. This might not come easy to you now, but don't give up, as one day you will look back and notice without judgment that kindness now comes naturally to you. It is no longer forced; the very act of kindness is just another part of your beautiful heart that you showcase naturally for the world to benefit from.

Life is just one big 'aha moment' that continually weaves together a multitude of 'aha moments' that are the culmination of snippets of your authentic Soul wisdom. Please don't make the same mistake that I made, spending years searching for the meaning of life. The truth is, if you are searching and searching and you never find the answers you are seeking for, you should stop looking. When you die, all of the spiritual answers will be available to you instantly. Instead of spending a lifetime on the existential questions maybe it is more important to spend our life living in the here and now? I believe our Soul purpose is to live life as a good human, and to love.

The wisdom that was shared in this book was only shared if I felt warmth in my heart, which told me that it is worthy of sharing. I hope you enjoyed reading this book. I can't thank you enough for this Soul journey that we have taken together, and from my heart to your heart… I send you love. Please remember, although human life is messy, raw, and often filled with far too much pain, when we begin to live and breathe virtues, we get the instant knowing that we are all on this walk of life together, and we are all heading to the same destination… so let's guide, help, encourage, and love each other.

It is my hope that you are always courageous enough to follow the calling of your Soul, and when you feel fear in the future you always fallback on your Soul. May the guiding grace of love, kindness, compassion, forgiveness, and gratitude create a foundation for you to have authentic happiness for your future. Go ahead and write a new story for the rest of your life, and make sure to include a million moments of love. Right now, your Soul is calling you to a familiar place of love. Please be brave enough to answer its call. You can be certain that when you live life with Soul, you will finally know what authentic happiness is.

> ***Soul-fueled Affirmation:** "I will always endeavor to use kindness as my weapon, love as my means of defense, hope as my fallback, and I will leave compassion as my calling card."*

Printed in the United States
By Bookmasters